Contents

PREFACE

Publishers would generally agree that putting the word 'Murder' on the cover of a book increases the chances of a sale. I wrote a book a few years ago about women killers in British history. As I researched it, I came across more and more sad cases of infanticide in the Regency and early Victorian years. To equate these killers with such murderers as Louie Calvert, boot fetishist and man-killer, seemed immoral. I didn't really want this to be a 'murder book' but it was published as *Yorkshire's Murderous Women* and I understand why.

The crimes of murder, rape and abduction, along with gangland antics and large-scale robberies, dictated the nature of the red and blacks on the true crime shelves for many years. But although they are still there, the spectrum has widened and there is more scope for the aspiring true crime writer now. The recent success of Kate Summerscale's *The Suspicions of Mr Whicher* show how the trend is for more ambitious, strong narrative books with a depth of enquiry into social history at the heart of the tale.

THE RED-BACK TEMPLATE

To a general reader, 'true crime' suggests books about the Krays, drug barons, bare-knuckle fighters with prison stories, and similar titles. But although the monthly magazines support that view in some ways, the first point to make is that any crime can be fascinating and multi-layered if the writer takes the research seriously. The market for the red backs is capable of being stretched because new crimes come along as society changes. The 'spree killer' phenomenon for instance, is an example. The names 'Hungerford' and Columbine' have a cultural resonance because the stories of these atrocities permeated the popular press and reasons for explaining such killings were explained by psychologists. Why a young man would walk into a high street and slay strangers at random is something to preoccupy a criminal profiler, but there is also an imaginative dimension, where a writer can be empathic and write almost semi-fictionally.

A crime writer can break that fixed template of murder and gangland by taking a different angle on the subjects, asking new questions, or revisiting the established opinions.

GENRES BROKEN DOWN

We live in an age when literary genres are transmuting and intermixing. Andrew Motion wrote a book on Wainewright, the poisoner, a man who really existed and moved in literary circles in the nineteenth century and who did poison people. But Motion made part of his book fictional, creating a productive and interesting mix of genres.

In writing true crime or crime history, the scope is there for including information from all kinds of areas and specialisms, such as medicine, psychology, political history, sociology and biology. After all, we live in a time when a botanist may find a valuable and rewarding career as a forensic botanist, coming out of the lab to work on a crime scene.

In the last few years there have been best-selling books on the shelves dealing with the first women convicts sent to Australia, the search for a great-grandmother who was imprisoned for murder after simply slackening her vigilance as she bathed her babies, body-snatching in Regency London and the East European crime outfits flooding British sex and drugs trades.

THE WRITER'S TOOLBOX

Just as detectives use the famous 'murder bag' invented by Sir Bernard Spilsbury, the crime writer needs a toolbox. This is my essential list, after six years of working as a true crime writer: a personal reference library, access to digital archives, newspaper cuttings files and a network of experts at archives and in organisations. My latest book will illustrate this. I have just completed *Cold Case Investigators* (Pen and Sword) which is a collection of cases solved by DNA sampling. Writing this was so much easier with the backup of my shelf of reference works on forensics and the newspaper archives on my computer. In addition, I had to check all kinds of facts, from place-names to legal professionals and work with journalists or archivists. These people have become acquaintances I can e-mail and ask regarding small details.

The writing after all this is a matter of knitting together a mass of facts and opinion. When I first started, I had to spend hours gathering these resources, but that has been invaluable. Writing at the screen, I have most of these sources and supports within arm's reach.

START WITH THE PEOPLE

Crimes happen for all kinds of reasons, and what was an offence in 1800 will not be one now. In 1950 suicide was still a criminal offence. Up to 1964 a person planning to take a life knew that one possible outcome of his act would be an appointment with the hangman. To help the true crime writer, there is an established 'classic structure' in the historical crime subjects: in the case of the 220 capital crimes on the statute books in Britain up to the 1820s, the structure of the narrative the writer follows is:

The crime and its circumstances
The pursuit and the arrest
The trial in court – or courts
The time in prison – the possibility of a reprieve or a commutation.
The execution

That may still be the basis of a successful book or article, of course, but my advice is to start with the people, not the offence. The best crime writing comes from the understanding and retelling of the human situation at the core of the story. Take the example of a man who has embezzled funds from some organisation for which he acts as treasurer. He has betrayed trust as well as broken the law. Understanding that human dilemma is an integral part of writing that story. The moral consequences are as important and intriguing as the legal ones.

PUBLICATION
Today, the long-established monthly true crime magazines are a good place to start. *True Crime, Murder Most Foul* and *True Detective* constantly need stories of course, and they invite well-researched stories, profiles and theories on all varieties of crime. The work involved in this kind of writing is an excellent basis for book-length work. Some subjects never fade away of course: any new angle on major subjects such as Jack the Ripper, The Moors Murders or Dick Turpin will always find a positive response. But equally, the sidelights of crime have a place too.

The first step is to reflect on exactly what aspects of crime and law interest you most profoundly. Some writers have the scientific interest needed for scene of crime and forensics writing; others prefer the intuitive writing required for such topics as psychopaths, deviancy and violent crime. But the range is vast, and crime borders on any number of other disciplines. In the course of writing my books I have had to understand political radicalism, the effects of various drugs, how arsenic may be detected and how detectives were trained in 1930.

If the story you choose has more questions than may be easily answered, then there is potential there. My own first writing in true crime was, I can now see with hindsight, an attempt to tell the bare events and bring in some social history. As I learned more, I worked hard to create layers of meaning and interest. That has enriched the whole process and of course, my satisfaction in the end product.

This handbook is intended to provide you with a guide, a route through the many sub-genres of this fascinating category of writing, a mix of social history, psychology and sheer instinct. When people ask where the 'creative' element in writing true crime lies, my response is usually that it lies in the feel for explanations of why we do extreme acts, why we 'lose it' and why, finally, the human being is a mystery, most of the time in balance, reserved, conformist, but beneath the exterior may lie a sea of discontent, resentment, rage, and even urges and desires that defy explanation.

1

THE TRUE CRIME GENRE

One-Minute Summary

'True crime' is perhaps not an ideal term to cover all the various versions of writing about crime and law that exist under the general category of what is now called 'creative non-fiction.' In some ways, the term 'Crime fact' is a more accurate term because the word true is a very moveable concept. What we see on the library shelves as 'true crime' always includes books that are really more usefully placed in other areas. But commercially, they are likely to be seen by the kind of readers who enjoy both contemporary and historical crime.

Clearly, the word 'true' was first used to distinguish writing about crime that actually existed to the made-up crime of crime fiction. But today, in a world of publishing and creative writing in which genres have blurred, these distinctions are of little importance. It is possible now to write about a fairly recent crime, for instance, by one of several methods relating to genre: historical, forensic, sensational or 'genre cocktail.' In the last category fact and fiction may mix. What we have now is a situation in which readers of the genre expect the sensational but also, with changes in the general knowledge of the public in relation to the professions linked to crime investigation, they also expect to be properly informed. In other words, the credentials of the true crime writer are of interest to the reader.

I gave a talk to a group of people in a large bookshop recently, and as the subject was crime history, I made a point of raising this issue. The fact is that some true crime writers are or have been professionals in the criminal justice system, but some are mere enthusiasts. That is an important distinction, but it does not necessarily mean that the amateur's writing will be of a lesser order.

But a summary of true crime writing must stress three central aspects of the genre: the domination of the gangland and prison books; the prevalence of murder above all other crimes as a subject, and the writer's position with regard to the subject. A useful example of how varied the writer's position may be is a glance at three books all dealing with life in a contemporary British prison. The writers of the three books might be: a convict, a prison officer and a criminologist, but each in his or her own way presents an angle on the prison today. They are all 'true crime' but in terms of film narrative, the convict's story will always be more impressive in a 'close up' sense, as if the camera is close to the subject. The other two versions will have varying degrees of distance from the prison life as seen from the prisoner, of course.

That example could be extended to any aspect of true crime. It is possible for a layperson to write about the police or about lawyers, for instance, but the results will be very different. In the end, this is an area of creative writing: true crime informs, uses empathy and describes worlds which the reader experiences vicariously. It stands as a successful genre on the fascinating standpoint from which we all ask questions about 'what is it like...' What is it like to be in a prison cell, be interviewed by police, steal from a bank, take a life, and so on. These questions of vicarious interest and empathy have been there from the start of the genre. A flick through the true crime magazines today shows that certain sub-genres dominate, and these all relate to the fascination with extremes of human wrong-doing: murder, execution, insanity and relationship crimes. The last one may have an everyday context such as the attack on a spouse, but may include such themes as cannibalism by consent or even the 2008 case of Josef Fritzl, the Austrian who imprisoned and raped his own daughter.

True crime genre, then, is really plural: it is more helpful to speak of the 'true crime genres.'

Historical Outline

What we now think of as true crime in English literature began with the stories of notable villains in *The Newgate Calendar*, stories collected in the early nineteenth century, but there had been chapbooks and ballads, cheap popular literature, sold in the streets and at executions for centuries. But it would not be too much of an exaggeration to say that ten Robin Hood ballads in the Middle Ages were also a variety of 'crime fact' mixed, naturally, with myth and legend. The Elizabethan prose writings dealing with thieves and robbers written by Thomas Nashe and Dekker clearly deserve a mention, in works such as Dekker's *The Gul's Hornebooke* (1609).

In the eighteenth century, John Gay's The Beggar's Opera (1728) is important in this context, dealing with thief takers and robbers. But the first real landmark in terms of modern true crime is arguably with Thomas De Quincey's long essay, *Murder Considered as One of the Fine Arts* in which the writer reflects on the popularity of murder for the general reading public and in the course of this refers to several contemporary stories. He gives a summary account of several famous murders in history, but then includes an account of the celebrated murders on the Ratcliff Highway by a man called Williams, and De Quincey writes:

'But one curious fact connected with this case I shall mention, because it seems to imply that the blaze of his genius absolutely dazzled

the eyes of criminal justice. You all remember… that the instruments with which he executed his first great work (the murder of the Marrs) were a ship carpenter's mallet and a knife.…this instrument (the mallet) Williams left behind him in the Marr's house.… But this circumstance of the publication of the initials
(carved on the tool) led immediately to the apprehension of Williams…'

De Quincey is writing with a reasoned response to the crime, asking pertinent questions, including details of the killings, and most important, he is aware of the readership and is in dialogue with those 'true crime' readers who could not resist a dramatic tale that led to the noose.

In the Victorian period, the expanding local press and the proliferation of regional newspapers led to the popularity of court and scaffold reports. A key publication here is *The Illustrated Police News* which had graphic line drawings of criminals, victims and lawyers, along with the scenes of crime of course. The emphasis was on sensation: up until 1868 there were public hangings in Britain, and the victims included women and children. That massive human interest was not lost on journalists and hack writers. Charles Dickens, among many other significant writers, was deeply interested in crime and mixed with some of the new London detectives after the formation of the detective force in 1842. His Inspector Bucket in *Bleak House* is the first detective in English fiction.

The twentieth century saw the introduction of more detailed and extensive works of true crime, many responding to the hugely infamous and celebrity-level murders such as those by Dr Crippen, Christie, Ruth Ellis and many others. Of course, the market for true crime had been increased dramatically after the Whitechapel murders of 1888 (Jack the Ripper), and the crook who had a taste for adventure and risk was a natural favourite with the public as well as with the press. From early in the twentieth century, the publishers, Hodge (and then others) published a series called *Notable British Trials* and these significantly expanded the interest in true crime, bringing in a wider readership.

A typical example of a 'pulp fact' series is the series called Mellifont Celebrated Crime volumes of the 1930s. A volume called *The Scaffold and the Dock*, for instance, is with a lurid red cover, showing a killer carrying the body of a female victim in a cellar, with the villain looking furtively behind him. In the book, by John G. Rowe, we have a mixed bag of crime stories, including 'a chapter of hangmen, other executions and scenes from the scaffold' and 'The Man they Could Not Hang.'

In the 1930s-1970s the nature of the genre consolidated into a literature dealing with the established subjects at the centre of interest: murder, hangings, detectives, sex crimes, massive robberies, gangland and courtroom drama. Police work was also to become more prominent as the activities of Scotland Yard became more high profile: by the 1960s there had been the formation of the Flying Squad, the Murder Squad and specialist groups such as Vice Squads and even the theme of terrorism and assassination. The latter was certainly not new: there had been at least four attempts on the life of Queen Victoria in the nineteenth century, and public figures of the stature of Churchill or the top generals were always in need of bodyguards.

To sum up, the development of true crime writing moved from short stories about highwaymen and outlaws to full-length narratives on the lives of villains or on court dramas. But something else came along too: biography began to emerge as a major part of the scene. Readers had always been interested in the lives of notorious criminals such as Dick Turpin or Jack Sheppard. But from the early twentieth century, there was a significant leap forward in this respect: a market for biographies of such figures as barristers and detectives or forensic scientists became prominent. Books from the underworld also did well, and prison memoirs. Clearly, in the days before television documentary, knowledge of life inside the walls of a prison or of a police station was slender in the public generally; the natural curiosity of people about the life of a detective, a burglar or a famous barrister was always there, eager for facts.

Today, the true crime genre has expanded and the spectrum was widened, with popular pot-boilers at one end, capitalising on red-hot news stories almost as soon as a trial has finished and a sentence given, to the literary, densely layered books dealing with community and social context in depth, such as *The Cruel Mother* by Sian Busby, dealing with a crime in her family history, or *Dick Turpin* by James Sharpe, telling the tale of the famous highwayman in a way that debunks the old myths. These recent works present a fascinating mixture of biography, social history and crime analysis, with the factual explanations always being integrated into the prose very deftly, so that there is popular appeal together with plenty of information. The true crime reader longs for important facts.

Choices before Writing

With all this in mind, it is easy to see that there has been a dominance of these varieties of books and articles in the true crime genre:

Gangland stories
Police investigations
Crime scene analysis
Execution tales
Prison memoirs
Bizarre and often explicit crime stories

Clearly, writers look for approaches that will include several of these. If a crime story involves virtually all elements of the full narrative of the crime, then the market interest increases. In fact, the classic narrative of crime-pursuit-trial-punishment still applies but with modern writing now being so sophisticated, there is plenty of scope to choose just one of the stages in the story of the crime and look at that in depth. For instance, it is quite possible to create a full and dramatic narrative merely from a police investigation. Take the case of a cold case murder: the killing may have taken place fifteen years ago, but there is DNA now available from the victim's garments. The ensuing chase, even though it may be a very slow, painstaking investigation, has a compelling appeal. After all, the detective has a wonderful scientific asset in his armoury now, with DNA sampling being possible from very poor material sources at murder scenes.

Some Examples
Broadly then, the choices open to the true crime writer now are these:
(a) Genres: the major 'red and black' crime fact books; biographies; historical narratives; documentary works, and crossover writing in which some other subject is mixed with a crime story, as in such books as those dealing with a personal slant on a major crime story.
(b) Specific categories: this is where the content becomes more important, so here is a basic list.

The casebook
This is a collection of short stories on crime cases, either by crime (obviously murder is dominant here) or by theme. So that there have been casebooks on, for instance, crime in Hollywood, or murders in theatreland etc.

Regional collections

Several major publishers run series on crime in particular areas, cities or counties. My own writing includes volumes in three of these series: *Foul Deeds and Suspicious Deaths* in... for Pen and Sword Books is typical of this. The aim here is to assemble around thirty crime stories over a period of time, and the titles hints at the breadth of subjects. For instance, in my book on Liverpool in that series, the stories included covered poisoning, murder, manslaughter, assault, fraud, robbery, burglary, obscenity and riot. The aim is to give the reader variety and also an insight into the changes in definitions of crime as time has passed. The term 'foul deeds' may be interpreted in many ways, and the trick is to include some crimes that are not violent, not 'crimes against the person' so that there will not be anything predictable, with one murder or serious assault following another.

Biographical Works

Ever more popular now, these books focus on one or more people, but also include the drama and excitement of the crime story, with the major events of that story as the spine of the narrative. A perfect example of this is *Four Against the Bank of England* by Ann Huxley (1969) in which Huxley tells the stories of the robbers and fraudsters with great skill and detail, while at the same time never wandering far from the challenge the crooks faced in working out a way to defraud the Bank of a vast amount of money in forged bills.

Thematic works

Of course, one particular aspect of crime and law may be used in a series. One such run of crime history books is on hangings. Three publishers currently maintain these series, with *Hanged at...* being an ongoing reference work with short accounts of executions at particular prisons. Obviously, the formula may be extended to any other subject such as 'infamous prisoners' and so on.

Thematic works might be extended to broader categories of course, such as trials or investigations, or even universal, global crime. A recent successful work in this area was *Killers* by Kate Kray, in which she spoke to and summarised the life and crimes of a series of killers, but the concept was to make the 'killers' in question people whose offences applied to an assortment of circumstances in which lives were taken. The result was a collection of profiles in which the reader discovered just what circumstances could lead to a killing.

It may be seen here just what a vast range there is in the notion of a 'theme.'

Single-Subject works

This is where the writing becomes ambitious, detailed and multi-layered. A typical example of this is the crime and life' mix of many American publishers who like to meet the market for a mass-market paperback story giving all the salient features of a criminal's life and the crime committed. A typical example would be the kind of book dealing with a shooting at a workplace: briefly: man with a grudge goes to workplace; he shoots and kills/maims colleagues; he then is arrested and tried. The book tells the back-story to that attack and adds a psychological profile of the perpetrator; friends and professionals are consulted for opinion and experience.

This may be extended into studies and stories of a specific crime rather than a person, or even a network of crime, such as the 2008 book *McMafia* by Misha Glenny, dealing with the impact of organised crime across Europe. Similarly, *The Trial* by Sadakat Kadri (2005) looks at 4,000 years of trials in society. One advantage of this approach is that the story reaches out to all categories of readers with a political interest also.

Reappraisals and Revisions

Few true crime books or articles can rival the never-ending appeal of the revision – the kind of book that looks again at a familiar or seemingly 'closed' case. Every year brings yet another such book on Jack the Ripper, with the latest expert putting forward a 'solution' to the mystery. But even more powerful because it is less common, is the kind of writing that has not only a new angle but new material. One of the most stunning pieces of writing in this respect is the recent (2008) discovery, with the use of mitochondrial DNA, that the body found in the cellar of Hilldrop Crescent was not the body of Mrs Crippen, Cora, for whose murder Crippen was hanged in November 1910 at Pentonville gaol.

Tutorial

The material covered so far indicates that this genre is one in the process of opening out and becoming something far more than the cheap shock thrillers of the crime magazines. The genre should appeal to writers who have a literary aspiration to produce something which mixes biography, discursive essay and cultural comment. But at the heart of the writing there is always some adherence to that classic format of crime- investigation- resolution. Some points to bear in mind are:

> ➢ A good true crime work will have a compulsive narrative, to compare with fiction
> ➢ Success depends on the right fusion of a people-story and a social context.

> Time must be taken to read and consider before the writing decisions are made
> Above all, acquire the habit of making organised notes and research processes from the start.

Whatever your outcomes and whatever effects you wish to communicate to the reader, the input will have to be more a strong, compelling narrative than a series of shocking episodes. The main danger in the genre is to oversimplify, so never be afraid to be an amateur lawyer/forensic scientist/ police detective. The reader knows that you are an enthusiastic amateur who loves to spin a tale from actual events and people's experience.

****

2

PLANNING AND RESEARCH

One-Minute Summary

True crime or crime fact, whatever label we use, are categories that are classified as one of the main areas of creative non-fiction. For that reason, the research and planning involved are as sound and methodical as the work done in areas such as history or geography. My own preparation for a new crime book entails this process:

(a)   A wide overview of existing thought and work in print.

(b)   A decision about what to include and what to leave out.

(c)   Ordering of events and ideas rated by importance

(d)   A summary of where and what the research resources are.

As with fiction, the story at the centre has to be one capable of intense emotional development. A simple starting-point is to consider, and contrast, two versions of a violent crime: one might be opportunist yet very nasty, leaving the victim fighting for life; the other might be premeditated, based on reasons which have been thought out, and the result may be the same for the victim. But of course there is an immense difference in terms of the writer and reader rapport and inherent interest in the story. A reason, a premeditation, means that there is a trajectory over a period of time, and in that time the offender and victim have some kind of relationship. That is your story, in its basic form.

But the research involved is always a mix of types. This is a check-list of sources used in one of my casebook stories which involved a servant girl who was charged and then acquitted for murder, back in 1870:

Newspaper reports
Court records
Social context – such as work, domestic situation and education etc.
The legal and police systems in place
The statute legislation and social attitudes

The girl in question was suspected of poisoning drinking water. The main reason for that suspicion was that she was known not to get on well with her employer, a farmer who was rough to her, and who made her work longer hours than she should have done. In other words, it was based on hearsay, and there were no other suspects.

But reading the first reports of the crime and the arrest, it was obvious, reading this, in 2009, that the death of the farmer may have been purely accidental, with adulteration of the water. That was almost certainly the case. But the girl had to go through the ignominy and stress of the questioning, the social ostracism, the court trial and the aftermath. She left town.

The main sources were the newspaper reports, but these are notoriously unreliable. For instance, in many cases place names have changed, legal terms have not been understood by the journalists, or there has been no scene of crime work.

Therefore, planning and research have to involve an understanding of the full picture before writing. In simple terms this is a three-stage process:

1. Gather all sources and write a chronology of events

2. Make character lists of the main protagonists in the tale
3. Summarise the legal process

If the subject is recent and you have people to talk to, then that adds a special dimension to the whole process. I once had a retired police officer helping me to assemble potential crime stories for a local book: he wrote to me with drawings and street plans, recalling the knowledge around the professional circles at the time.

Questions to Start With

In research, the questions often start with 'where?'

As with a novel, a good true crime story starts with questions – mainly about the human motivation implicit in the case. Why did the person commit the crime? That is merely the central, obvious one. But consider such complex questions as, 'Why did the killer hate the victim so much that the body had a cigarette burn stubbed on the belly? Why would the criminal attack in the open, seen by witnesses? Why would a death be made to seem like suicide? On and on the questions arise, just as they do in detective novels and dramas.

The first questions should be about the relation between the crime and (a) society or community and (b) the criminal and the victim. Here is an example from my case files.

(a) The crime

A police officer, in the late Victorian times, was found dead by the roadside. He had been shot. Earlier that day, it was discovered, a local farmer had been told by the police officer to move his cart, which was left outside a pub, illegally placed. The farmer was arrested and questioned. He confessed after being pressed to explain matters and also where he had spent his day.

(b) The research

This is such an easy, one-dimensional tale. You could tell the crime story in one page. But that is without research. In this case, the research is in the community and in the nature of the dead man of course. Local crime records would tell you that the killer had been in court before, for petty crimes, and that the police officer was involved in those prosecutions. It all seems like a clear-cut case: vengeance. The worm turned. The bullying man with power finally went too far and the man without power had enough of what he saw as victimization.

But that is all legal. What if the dead man was suspected of having an affair with the killer's wife? Then we have a moral dimension. Once again, the legal and the moral have power to claim attention.

Sources: Primary

A primary source is information from the time of the event, either from participants or from observers. It may be a paper source in an archive or it may be a statement by a person, talking from memory. In the case of Jack the Ripper, for instance, there were people who almost certainly saw Jack on the nights of some of his murders. They spoke to police and their words were recorded. Then there were other professionals involved. A basic list of primary sources for those famous 1888 Whitechapel murders might look like this:

Recorded statements of neighbours and passers-by

Written police records
Reports by medical men
Drawings of the bodies
Street plans and maps

Letters/correspondence (written by all kinds of people, and some perhaps from Jack himself, although that is now generally not thought to be so)

Obviously, as with all historical study, there is bias, misapprehension, vested interest and so on, in all these sources.

Primary sources need to be studied closely. Even a short statement can give much information for the writer. For instance, in 1840 there was an attempt on the life of Queen Victoria. A poster printed at the time gives a short report of this, including this passage about the young man who tried to do the deed:

'On being taken to the station-house, he gave his name EDWARD OXFORD, a native of Birmingham, 17 years of age, and lived as a pot-boy at the Hog-in-the-Pound, Marylebone Lane, facing Oxford Street, and that he lived in a room at No. 6 West Street... on searching of which the police found a sword and a black crepe cap made to fit the face, a powder flask and bullets which fitted the pistol...'

The boy was considered to be insane and so did not hang. As a primary source, this statement invites us to look into both the circumstances of his low, poor life, and also into the mind that made the materials of his appearance when he made the attack. In other words, the questions go outwards into society and inwards into the personality.

All good true crime stories have the triangular interplay of those items: society- crime-personality of the criminal. Sometimes the personal dimension is the reason for the crime and so social elements are merely secondary, and sometimes the crime has an open, public, very social dimension (like an assassination or a riot) and so the personality may not be of great interest.

Ideally of course, an article or book will be enriched if there is a balance of solid paper source material and a degree of anecdotal or oral-historical source material. In the course of writing an article for a crime magazine I once talked with some long-term prisoners and we wandered onto the subject of a certain multiple killer who several men there had met in gaol. One story told was that the man strapped copies of *Country Life* magazine around his torso as a defence against knife attacks. That kind of detail adds to the available elements of the narrative already in the printed books.

A primary source may be something very minute –something apparently of little value until a link to something much more significant occurs. For instance, I was once researching crime in Liverpool and I was working on the riots and attacks on German property and people in the aftermath of the sinking of the *Lusitania* in May, 1915. By sheer serendipity, I came across a collection of interviews in an old magazine, and this included stories given to a researcher by people who witnessed some of these attacks. To add to that, in a trade publication from the shipping lines, I found the deeply ironical advert for the company who fitted out that vessel: apparently it was fitted with Howden's patent forced draught installations. This was something of no use whatsoever against a torpedo of course.

What tends to happen in crime research is that a cluster of different reference sources with gather – even around one chapter in a case book. This is a typical example of one chapter, in my book, *Foul Deeds and Suspicious Deaths in Bradford.*

Chapter: The Lozenge Poisoning Case 1858

Main narrative: the accidental inclusion of arsenic in the recipe for sweet manufacture – caused by a mistaken collection by a worker with low literacy.

Inherent knowledge. The nature of collective responsibility and negligence in law at the time / master and servant responsibility / civil suits for a tort (rather than a criminal offence).

Secondary knowledge. The nature of the materials used in the sweet-making (e.g. a mixture called 'daff' (terra alba); medical effects of arsenic poisoning / the geography and communications involved.

It may be seen from this that the inherent knowledge – what you need to know from the reported story itself – is just the beginning of your work. You must add to that the range of secondary knowledge required , and this may be from all kinds of areas of expertise. The writer has to knit together the drama of the tale, the legal elements and the more day-to-day aspects of the social history. Usually the understanding of the local community is the key to sorting out the real interest in the crime story.

This naturally brings up the issue of reference works, and so we move on to secondary sources.

In terms of the more straightforward historical work involved in researching true crime, we have the ample resources of the archives. The foundation of this is a knowledge of the various criminal courts in the systems over the centuries if there is an historical perspective in the work planned. A watershed in this is the establishment of crown courts in 1970. Before that, the research involves looking for the right court in the various circuits on which judges sat at assize courts. This can be complex. For example, a trial which would normally be heard at Lincoln may have been held at Nottingham, or at one period, trials previously held at York were shifted to Leeds when the assizes were rationalised in the Victorian years.

But basically, the sources which will be useful in researching a crime and trial process are these:

Quarter sessions records at country record offices
Assize courts records either at The National Archives or sometimes in the provinces.
Newspaper reports of crown court trials since 1971.
The Old Bailey session papers (online)
Other courts depending on the offence and on the period in question.
There will be full explanation of this in the next chapter.

Secondary sources

The material you need in printed materials is diverse. It is wise to begin with a personal reference collection, and this is my basic list for the crime writer:

A dictionary of law

There are several, but my personal favourite is *Osborn's Concise Law Dictionary* edited by Mick Woodley.

A dictionary of British History

The two most useful are *The New Penguin Dictionary of Modern History* and *The Oxford Dictionary of British History.*

A dictionary of social history

This is likely to be in various forms. The classic Brewer's *Dictionary of Phrase and Fable* has a wealth of information. But more modern, and excellent for all kinds of reasons, is *The Sutton Companion to Local History* by Stephen Friar.

A crime fact encyclopaedia

The best paperback example is out of print as I write this, but second-hand copies are not hard to find: Oliver Cyriax's *The Penguin Encyclopaedia of Crime* (last updated in 1996)

Biographical reference for crime and law

There is no recent single volume for this. But second-hand anthologies of 'Great Judges' help, and there is a very useful recent collection on criminals: *Rogues, Villains and Eccentrics* by William Donaldson.

A history of police

The standard work is by Clive Emsley: *The English Police.*

A medical encyclopaedia

The perennial favourite, *The Penguin Medical Dictionary* will suffice.

A work on forensic science

Many of these are very technical and are a tough read for someone with no solid foundation knowledge in the terminology of biological science. But Brian Lane has come to the rescue with his fine work, *The Encyclopaedia of Forensic Science.*

Most of these will be works still in print, but some of the best in some categories are not. As I have indicated, the out-of-print works may be available from specialist booksellers, and these are listed in my own reference section. All of the above are listed with full bibliographical details at the end of this book.

Secondary sources for true crime are often most valuable when they involve memoirs and biographies. For instance, although the newspapers have lots of information on specific modern crimes, the autobiographies usually come after the events and these usually have information that has not been available before. This is particularly true of high-profile crimes such as serial murders. In these cases, the writing by the victims or relatives of victims is almost always of great value to the writer. Of course, there has been a glut of 'villain memoirs' and these have been immensely successful. The writings of Frank Fraser are a typical example. His books involve personal anecdotes and sidelights on many well established events and people's lives and crimes.

Categories of secondary sources are in a very wide spectrum, going from memoirs to interviews with criminals, documentaries, forensic analyses, to accounts of victims and even extreme perspectives such as 'confessions' by people who were involved in crimes which are now 'safe' territory in that the participants have all died. The market in true crime for the central, firmly established topics of the Krays, London gangland, prison celebrities and 'white collar' scams never goes away. One publisher once wrote that a writer wanting to burst into print need only consider the market for books on Sherlock Holmes, Jane Austen and the Brontes to realise that some subjects exist for which the 'market research' in unnecessary because the readership is constant and never goes away. This arguably applies solidly to the above true crime genres.

Tutorial

This chapter has stressed that research in true crime entails a substantial amount of foundation knowledge. Basically, this knowledge reflects the criminal justice system in place at the time of the crime, in addition to the wider frame of reference as the world changes.

With the understanding of the nature of sources, together with a reference collection (and of course the internet) the crime writer can easily put together a research base for writing. The skill then comes in the process of selection and rejection of material. But this is only a gradual process; the more the writer uses sources, the quicker the action of sorting becomes. A good filing system is the answer, so that various types of information may easily be integrated into an article or into a chapter. All this may be summarised in this way:

(a)   Decide on what knowledge is needed for the case

(b)   Find the best sources

(c)   Understand what is needed from those sources

(d)   Relate the new material to what you already have

(e)   Integrate everything within the basic spine of the crime narrative.

3

THE ELEMENTS OF THE CRAFT I

One-Minute Summary

It might come as a surprise to some readers to learn that true crime, contrary to much popular belief, is not merely something that concerns pot boilers that cash in on hot news. It is easy to see where that idea comes from. In the bookshops as I write this there are books on two major crimes and criminals which are only just completed in terms of the trial process and sentencing; it is as if the genre of true crime works like the obituary – writing ready to be delivered on the instant that there is news. That common perception takes some shifting.

But, as explained in the preface, today there is very much a more consciously literary element in much true crime, especially that which relates to history or to social or biological science. Within that writing, there is room for the imagination, and even semi-fictional prose. This chapter looks at some of the skills involved, and I am using a case study, but first, here is a check list of skills – those relating directly to the writing craft.

The sense of structure

In true crime, the choices of the order of presentation are still, there, as they are in fiction or in such genres as life-writing. The story has to be assembled and then told in an order that will create a reader rapport. A traditional option for the opening, for instance, is the in media res approach – literally 'in the middle of things' – so that the tale starts with the crime itself perhaps.

The legal foundations

Clearly, the knowledge of law and criminology described in the last chapter is relevant here: it has to be seamlessly introduced into the prose narrative.

The crime itself

Decisions have to be made about how the crime is to be explained, how it is best 'given' to the reader. This always involves a notion of what might be called 'heavy' and 'light' writing: this about decisions regarding the amount of factual detail introduced.

Contextual Matter

Conversely, how much parallel information is needed and of what kind? There is always the urge to explain and that may be followed by over-explaining (hence the 'heavy' prose).

Legal Knowledge

Obviously, every crime story involves some aspects of law as they existed at the time of the offence. That therefore entails all kinds of matter, such as these topics:

Lawyers and barristers/ the nature of defence/ statute law and precedent/ expert witness testimony, and so on. This case study will show the skills involved in such writing. The following is a short account of a crime that incorporates discussion of a statute. It is the kind of article that might be written simply to show how one small incident can open up wide discussion and also give the reader something to reflect upon.

A Vagrancy Issue 1955
' ... the mere sight of the document would show that the appellant was a man with a long list of convictions...'

The problem of homeless drifters has been a nagging problem for English law since the first poor laws and vagrancy statutes of the Elizabethan period, but by the 1950s, tramps, drifters and generally suspicious looking types were a thorn in the flesh in a different way. A case in Grimsby highlighted the difficulties of dealing with this.

In English criminal law, a person standing charged with an offence has to be tried on the grounds of that specific offence, and nothing else beyond that. Courts in the past have often run into trouble and made mistakes because of contravening that rule. In the case of a known criminal in Grimsby a mistake was made.

In October, 1955, Mr Fitzwalter Buller found himself acting for a group of people whose property had been under threat from a 'vagrant' named Fuller. It was going to be a simple matter to show that the man had been up to no good on some premises, as the recorder at the quarter sessions in Grimsby had been given a long list of the man's previous convictions. That was a step that the aggrieved parties may have regretted because the case went to the court of appeal.

It was a case of a record of a known 'bad character' being given in court to prejudice a decision. Fuller had been asked why he had not accepted work, as he had not appeared in court at an earlier time. Then, on the night in question, he had been found in a place where he was almost certainly going to commit an offence.

The drifter was a man who had caused a series of confrontations with the local police and he was often under observation; it was known that he was the type who could easily shift from minor offences to other, more serious ones, and when he was caught and charged on this particular occasion, that thinking lay behind the police actions. but it was in the court that things went wrong for everyone concerned, and all because of a too enthusiastic court officer.

Fuller had been given a three-month prison sentence for that offence, under the old Vagrancy Act of 1824, so there was a feeling of certainty that he was out to do a burglary or even worse. But, as the appeal court noted, to haul him up in court and then place the list of convictions in from of the judge was malpractice. The judge at appeal said, 'The merest glance at the report by anyone accustomed to that class of document, as every recorder would be, would show him that he was dealing with what might be called 'an old hand.' The mere sight of the document, it was said, would show that the appellant was a man with a long list of previous convictions.

The outcome was that if there was an appeal against a conviction, then no details of previous convictions should be made visible. The man had gone to prison on what in legal terms is called an 'unsafe' judgement. Clearly, this all became a matter of prejudice, and that was not difficult to show before the High Court Judge, Mr Justice Ormerod.

Here was a case of a 'bad character' who nevertheless found himself languishing in gaol because he had received a 'punishment' for thing s allegedly done well before the latest appearance in court. Maybe his defence in court - that he had been on the property when he was arrested looking for work – did not really convince the magistrate, but he was badly handled, and that was the bottom line.

The fateful list, given to the Recorder, could not have been put in front of a jury, and so a basic principle of law had been breached. The basis of the debate was in the operation of the so-called 'Sus laws' and these were common causes of discontent at the time. The famous detective Jack Slipper, on the streets at the same time as the Grimsby event, has this to say about these laws which enabled officers to stop anyone 'on suspicion': 'As I became more experienced I had a number of good arrests, thanks to the Section Four of the 1824 Vagrancy Act which allows a police officer to arrest someone he suspects of being about to commit an arrestable offence. That doesn't mean you can pick up someone just because he might be a criminal...'

In other words, the Grimsby affair happened largely because the officers concerned knew the man in question. He was not 'just someone.'

Basically, this shows how examination of the 1824 Act created a problem. The skill involved here is the balance of precise, official language and the approachable vocabulary of the everyday: such as using the quote from Jack Slipper alongside the judge's expression. The basis of this is the difficulty of working with rather out-dated legislation. In 2008 the Law Commission set about reporting on obsolete laws such as the 1972 Servants' Characters Act which set out to sort out the wrongs of false character references. There has been only one case of giving false references in the courts. In the above story, everything hinges on the man Fuller and the immediate social context, so really, under the legal discussion, he is the focus, and that human element counts for most in the end.

The legal knowledge needed by a true crime writer falls into three categories: first, the explanations required in the text; second, the general legal notions to be applied and third, the use of legal information in the texture of the writing.

Explanations in the text
A classic example is the use of a technical term in the source material. An example of this that always occurs in historical crime writing is *habeas corpus.* This literally means 'you are to have the body.' This is a writ that requires someone to be brought to court to stand before a

judge. The main aim in times past was to determine the lawfulness of that person's detention. Therefore, in times of political fears, such as when treason, sedition or mutiny –or even rioting – were feared, habeas corpus could be suspended, meaning that a person could be condemned *in absentia* – while not being there to speak or answer for him or herself. This enlargement on the meaning would have to be explained. Luckily, we have a handbook to help – *Lawyers' Latin* by John Gray (see bibliography).

General legal notions
While writing, some legal concepts are not only in need of explanation, but actually figure in the drama of the story. An example is the simple word *alibi*. Again, this is Latin, meaning simply 'elsewhere.' In the context of a full work in true crime, this might occur in the main story, but the interest in the idea is how the police treat such a thing as opposed to how the defence lawyer might, or how a witness might, treat the event concerned.

Legal writing in the texture of words
This is the creative element. Suppose you want to include a legal principle in the drama, then you might have this: 'There was no thought of what meanings might be found later in that swinging of the hammer towards the victim's skull; no words inside his head muttered *intention* as the weapon fell mercilessly and crashed into bone. That simple word evokes the basic idea in law of a criminal intent, of a *mens rea* in a murder case – a 'criminal intent.'

Criminal Histories
This particular skill is related to reading and a chosen style. Basically, when a writer reads there is an intertextual play of influence. You want

to tell a story in your way: but all the previous reading means that you have learned, without thinking, how the genre works, and in your chosen technique. Consequently your writing style will be somewhere on the spectrum from 'heavy' to light' in terms of the density of the writing. At the centre of this is the criminal history itself and how you relate that. Compare these sentences for instance:

(a) It was decided that the accused should not speak in court. The defence team considered that the defendant's manner, lack of education and slightly suspect delivery (caused by a mental trauma) would be detrimental to the case, and so the man, shivering with fear in the court cell, was strongly advised to remain silent, especially in the dock.

(b) The accused man stood silent through the trial, being told that he should simply watch ad listen, keeping in control, while they knew he was breaking up inside.

It is all about degrees of emotional writing and levels of factual, informative 'weight.' The old-fashioned crime writing was heavily sensational in some hands, and that still has a place. But today we live with layers of complexity in the court process and in professional mind-games in the participants.

It is useful to reflect that there are arguably certain established ways of writing a true crime story: factual, documentary and imaginative. Each requires a certain mix of skills of course. They might best be described in this way:

Factual
Based on the assumption that many readers of the genre enjoy the details of the elements involved, from police to forensics and the

court of law, this approach revels in the minutiae of such things, so that there will be meticulous accounts of the police involved for instance, and of the nature of the scene of crime.

Documentary

This uses the factual basis but takes time over the key events, so that for example, most stress is on the significance of the spine of the story, following motivation for the offence, vividness in describing the professionals involved, and in giving important statistics.

Imaginative

This is the traditional, sensational approach but with a modern voice, perhaps playing around with the time sequence or including speculative passages, evoking the community around the scene of crime and so on.

But at the heart of the techniques for this genre is the basic template, which may be written briefly, as in this example concerning a Victorian crime in Yorkshire; it shows the basic elements of a 'crime fact' story, as opposed to the modern 'true crime' as we think of it. The framework of events is there, with only a bare commentary on the larger world around the crime:

FISHERMAN WITH A GUN
Richard Insole   21 February, 1887

Mr Justice Field, a judge very busy on the Midland Circuit, arrived in Lincoln for the Assizes in 1887 fresh from a number of murder trials on the 'road' as a busy judge. He was well-known for his tough, no nonsense attitudes to the implementation of the worst sentences of the law, and now he was to preside over the trial of a Grimsby man. He was then seventy-four and age had certainly not softened his character; he had not been called to the Bar until he was thirty-seven and it could be said that he was determined to make his mark. In his long career he was involved in several high-profile cases and the small matter of yet another working man who murdered his wife was not going to trouble him.

Mr Harris, defending the accused, Richard Insole, knew that he had a difficult task. It was an uncomplicated case. Insole, a fisherman, had been separated from his wife Sarah since July the previous year; she had gone back to live with her parents and was earning a wage. Insole had a set intention to take her life, such was his hatred of her. He bought a revolver and cartridges on the 7 of January, 1887 and at around ten in the morning, he appeared at Sarah's parents' home. He went in and started a row.

The couple had a furious interchange of anger and accusation, and eventually Insole fired a shot at his wife, but she managed to raise a hand and knock his hand so that the bullet went high and wide of her. But the man was determined and he shot again, that time hitting her in the chest and she fell back into a chair. He was still not finished, as he fired again but that time deciding to fire into the floor instead. Insole saw in that split-second that there was no going back – still in a rage he was interrupted by the arrival of his wife's mother who he shoved roughly away before putting the barrel of the gun next to Sarah's heart and firing twice. She died almost instantly, of course, and he ran off. Insole was tracked down without any difficulty and at his own home he was arrested and detained.

His defence lawyer argued that Insole had been desperately jealous and in that state had been totally distracted and not at all his normal self. As The Times reported the case, Harris had admitted defeat really, as he said that 'he could not contend that there were any circumstances which would reduce the offence to manslaughter' and that he still (very

40

pathetically really) thought that the introduction of the notion of jealousy would help the jury see his client in 'a favourable light'. He was backing a loser. Yet it must be recorded that Harris's speech achieved one thing: it guided the jury to suggest a recommendation for mercy after a guilty verdict. They had been convinced by the account of Sarah's affair with another man.

But Mr Justice Field was ready with his black cap again. His jury had actually used the word provocation when they asked for mercy. In 1887 that was a word with no weight at all in a case where a killer had patently had a planned intention to take life. He bought the gun and bullets, went to Sarah's home, roughly assaulted her mother, and fired the gun with a definite intention to kill. The deaths sentence was passed on him and Justice Field did repeat the recommendation to mercy, but it was, as he well knew, futile.

In Grimsby, however, a sufficiently large number of people felt that they should sign a petition to save Insole's life. On 12 February, that petition was noted in the newspapers: 'A petition is being signed that the capital sentence passed upon Richard Insole the Grimsby murderer be commuted to penal servitude for life.' It was fruitless and on Monday, 24 February at the new prison on Greetwell Road, Lincoln, the Bradford executioner James Berry arrived to see Insole into the next world.

In Berry's memoirs, a book in which many of his victims were given a few pages of detail regarding their exits, it is noticeable that Richard Insole had no more than a few basic words. The fact he wishes to note is that Insole fired the gun for the last time as she was lying on the ground; he must have formed an opinion of the killer so low that he took a certain pleasure in hanging Insole that day in Lincoln.

James Berry had another appointment the next day, in Nottingham, where another young wife-killer was waiting to step up the scaffold to the very professionally prepared noose. This was Benjamin Terry – a man sentenced by Mr Justice Field, who was so accustomed to putting on the black cap that one pathetically distracted Grimsby fisherman was just one more face in front of him who deserved to die.

Background

The degree to which the social context should be included is a debatable one. There are various levels of factual or imaginative writing that relate to the extent of social commentary the individual case needs, in order that your reader grasps the import of the case fully. For instance, it might be useful to consider what elements of background generally figure in a crime story. This summary provides a useful explanation of possibilities:

First, the *immediate context:* family, street, local historical considerations. This deals with the relations between the killer/ victim and those immediately around them. If a crime takes place in a particular industry for instance, or in a tight-knit community, then the moral structures of that community will be the first concern. An example might be a crime committed in a workplace for instance – in the modern world, perhaps a spree killing such as the 'high school mass murder' phenomenon mainly in the USA.

Then there is the level of background that introduces the *larger subjects and questions* such as a whole industry or regiment or profession, as the case may be. The story will need explanations of social relations, status and other aspects. A good example of this might be a police killing or a murder in a duel. In each of those two examples, we can see how there would be repercussions across a specified sub-culture or occupational group.

Finally, there is the *theoretical angle,* bringing in social and medical science perhaps. A good example is a case involving serial murder, as that clearly invites knowledge and theory on the specific habits and modus operandi of the killer. It might involve reference to offender profiling or to 'crime-mapping.' Of course, a crime narrative of some length may mix all of these. A typical book on a major true crime subject, such as Jack the Ripper, will have all of these and possibly more. But these examples make a useful foundation for reflecting on choices for writing, at the planning stage of the book.

Tutorial

No matter which approach is chosen for your story, the point is that you will write to your strengths and interests: that will generally emerge in the process of research, and that is why time taken over exploring and considering sources is so important. A crime done with planning, intent and cold-blooded state of mind is radically different from, say, a violent attack done in the heat of a family argument. As there are so many circumstances around each individual crime, the demands made on the writing treatment will be diverse, giving the writer a great deal of choice in style, vocabulary and narrative voice.

A simple way to see this is to note that in 1957, as the abolition of hanging was being debated in Britain, a report of enquiry added an appendix to its material: this was a list, with brief descriptions, of fifty murders committed in one year during the writing of that report. Each short paragraph describing the murders showed just what a wide spectrum is applicable here. One example was a man who had been very drunk, set about his friend with his fists, intending to do harm, and the friend died. In contrast, another death was an assault by a gang on one victim that went beyond the intention of 'a good hiding' and resulted in the victim dying. The crime story you construct will be, in the last resort, a compelling narrative, regardless of techniques chosen and skills applied.

4

THE ELEMENTS OF THE CRAFT II

One-Minute Summary

We are now at the point at which it is useful to discuss the basis of true crime – the reason for its success and appeal. At the root of the story there is the notion of transgression – the fantasy of imagining what it is like to transgress the laws of a state but also the moral laws that supposedly rule 'civilised' behaviour. In simple terms, there is empathy: the daring question of 'I wonder what it is like to take life/ steal thousands of pounds / be hunted by detectives and so on. Some of the best insights, to be used by the writer, are to be found in the best villain memoirs, particularly those in which a crime is indeed overtly a 'moral' as well as a criminal one.

A useful example is the crimes resulting from adultery. Almost every week there is a news story concerning a man or woman who have injured or even killed someone 'for love.' In other words, for the opening up of the illicit pleasures of an affair into centre stage. What has been secret, covert, underhand, becomes known. That is the second thrill: the changed perceptions of the person who has committed a crime 'for love' or even for 'lust' of course.

The French idea of the *crime passionel*, the 'crime of passion' is a very clear instance of this true crime interest. A person decides that the only way to happiness with the new partner is to remove the present partner from the scene: that would be a terrible murder. But on a lower level, if say a woman who is beaten or mentally bullied finds happiness in the arms of another man and turns on her oppressor – intending to warn or frighten, not to kill. There is a real story of course: something packed with complex motivations and which invites all kinds of moral judgements from the reader.

This chapter is also concerned with how to write these kinds of stories in different ways. We look at taking certain stances and at presenting the elements of the tale in differing ways. Then, at the heart of a true crime story, there is the question of atmosphere: mental, material or even imaginative.

Micro and Macro Focus

First, before any explanation, here is a short crime story. Read and consider what kinds of selection of material and telling have been done.

Charlotte Barton: The Hammer Murder

In the Victorian period, a high proportion of people cohabited, and especially in the industrial towns, where strict moral rectitude was perhaps less of a problem for a couple with regard to the immediate neighbours. It often made practical sense to have a younger woman 'living in' and being basically a mix of wife and 'domestic.' The story of Charlotte Barton, however, highlights some of the problems with these arrangements when things go wrong.

Thomas Padgin was fifty-seven and he worked as a shoemaker. Before the fateful events of December 1870, they had lived together reasonably happily for twelve years. The Police News report says that they were known as 'quiet people' and that Charlotte kept a respectable house, taking pride in her housework. Padgin was described as 'elderly in the report, but that was perhaps partly related to the life expectancy of the time, and partly to the fact that he was ill. Although in his youth

45

he had been sturdy and well, for some years before these events, he had suffered from a paralysis; he was unable to hold down a job and luckily he had finance coming to him from friendly societies and welfare clubs. But it does seem, reading between the lines of this horrible tale that he was short of cash.

On Tuesday 8 December, 1870, Charlotte snapped. She set about her partner with an intent to kill him, and the poor police constable who was sent to the house would have cast his eyes on very little that was unusual until he reached the steps leading down to the cellar. There, lying across some steps, was the body of Padgin, bent double, with the head pointing down the stairs. The corpse was mutilated, and it was later found that in no less than seven places there were severe injuries which had caused broken limbs or joints. It was a scene of carnage: a pool of blood had gathered at the foot of the stairs and in a little sink there was more blood. The Police News report notes that 'The body was removed to the upstairs room and laid on a couch. One eye was upturned, the other closed up, and shockingly bruised. The face on both sides was pounded into a mass of pulp and the head was dreadfully mangled.'

Why this had happened is a complex question, though Charlotte's explanation to her brother when she went to see him after the killing was simple enough. Her reason was, 'He wanted me to go with other men.' The fact that she made strenuous efforts to clean up after the crazed attack suggests a deeply troubled mind. She apparently scrubbed clean most of the surfaces that had been spattered with blood, and she had tried to take stains off walls, though without real success.

In court, at the inquest, the killer gave some surprising facts or perhaps half-truths. She said that her husband was still living nearby, at Broad-Lane, and that she had in fact married Pagdin. But her mind was disintegrating, because when she was quizzed about this apparent bigamy, being asked if she had two husbands living she said, 'No, only one.'

The facts of the attack she had erased from her mind, and at the trial in Leeds, she denied using the axe in the attack. Willful murder was the charge, and a crowd of friends and relatives appeared and showed much concern. The case was reported as being a tale of 'an unfortunate woman' not a crazy axe-murderer, and so it seems. The sentence was the humane one: that Charlotte Barton was a lunatic, and was therefore unfit to plead. It was a sad case of incarceration in an asylum. It appears that the reality of what was happening to her never really sank in, as she kept a 'cool and indifferent demeanour' throughout the inquest and the trial itself.

Beneath the horrible bare facts of this murder there perhaps lies another story, something bound up inextricably with the couple's changing relationship under duress as the financial hardships set in, and the hint about her being asked to earn money by prostitution, however bizarre and deranged that might have seemed when stated, could well have a kernel of truth. It would have been the kind of pressure put upon a woman in those hard times well before the welfare state and at a time when the fear of the ultimate fall – the workhouse – was for many a genuine terror to be avoided at all costs.

When the woman walked to her brother's shop and said simply, 'I have hit Pagdin with a hammer' is was surely a terrifyingly downbeat statement, as if talking into a mirror, expressing a piece of reality that was too hard to bear.

Notice that the story was linked almost at every stage to broader contextual subjects and issues. But this is really only the kernel of the tale: several aspects of this could be developed, but of course they involve speculation and commentary. These are matters such as the nature of the central relationship, the terrible resonance of her statement that 'he wanted me to go with other men,' and her behaviour at the trial.

I always think of the essential details of the relationship in any crime as the 'micro' focus and the interest of the bigger questions as a 'macro' focus. In other words, it would be possible to tell this story almost entirely in terms of the world of prostitution in working class communities at the time (1870) and giving only the bare details of the specific people involved. Conversely, a micro focus would be a genuine 'people story.'

Returning to the topic of transgression: notice how there are degrees of this, and the adjective usually give away the moral perspective in the contemporary setting: words such as 'heinous' or barbaric' clearly invite the reader to adopt a shared social view. But an open word such as 'tragic' may invite speculation about a transgression and the motivations behind it.

Micro writing is about the inward nature of people – intensely concerned with motivation; macro writing is about the community as a focus for morality, causality and judgment. A clear example of how macro writing may be used is in riots and disorder or in war crimes. In these public acts of criminality there will always be a plain, often well established reason for the transgressions of both criminal law and morality. But in writing about a riot for instance, the writer will have plenty of scope for describing the causes that led to the disorder, and so the metanarrative of the 'spirit of the age' or of the economic structures will be possible. I was once writing about the crimes committed in the age of body snatching (mainly the Regency years) and in the early 1830s, when there was an epidemic of cholera in many English cities and towns, the body snatchers would have plenty of cadavers to snatch and sell; but one consequence of this was that gangs of relatives would gather at hospitals where family members lay ill, and they would stand watch and vigil in case there was a death and the 'resurrection men' would arrive, like hyenas around a corpse. Would a physical assault on a suspected body snatcher be a serious crime?

A Feeling for Atmosphere

Of course, the crime scene is of great importance. But that bland, overdone phrase needs to be theorized a little. The place where a crime takes place may be of interest to a writer for all kinds of reasons. As forensic analysis will reveal, there is always some kind of hint about a psychological profile in a place. It may be anything from an arena of combat to a place of extreme fear. The link between the offence and the material reality of the place itself may contain the most telling narrative of the events in question. In writing, the place has potentially three types of presence in the crime story:

Somewhere chosen, with significance.

A communal location

Lives in transit

In the first, the criminal is 'playing at home' and there is control of circumstances and all the items present. In writing the story of a crime, this may be the springboard to the whole story, as in the obvious example of Dennis Nilsen, the serial killer who 'killed for company' and who kept the bodies of victims close to him.

The second is about the criminal as a perceived member /outcast of a community: his crime will relate to that status or lack of status. Consider how many crime fictions have been made around the idea of an outsider or someone forced 'outside' a community who has a grudge or a deep hatred. But again, crimes against one who has transgressed a communal ideological morality are common, and the place in question may be of significance with that in mind.

49

Finally, the idea of crimes 'on the move' covers opportunist crimes, as in random murders and rapes for example, where the opening up of the criminal opportunity is often related to anonymity. If victim and assailant are 'in transit' – rootless, one of the crowd, then anything is possible in the fantasy behind a criminal act. This is why assaults by people in uniform present opportunist anonymity. The criminal act was done 'by a man in uniform' – any one of hundreds of course. Or 'the killer was a tramp.'

Throughout history, before a professional police force, imagine how terrifying the black night was: one's property, family and land were open to attack and rapine by anyone who could exploit your vulnerability in the night. The first attempts at civic protection came from 'watch and ward' – the personnel appointed to supervise the streets for lawlessness: the ward by day and the watch by night. The criminal on the loose, like the outlaw or the highwayman, the mugger or the footpad, presents the writer with descriptions of place that evoke a whole lifestyle and a fascinating transience – today, the typical urban attack, by the powerful on the vulnerable.

Sequencing events

In any narrative, the decisions made by the writer about how the events are to be told are very important. The established methods of maximizing effects by carefully ordering the sequence of events for the reader are well known. Basically the choice is between a plain chronological account with embellishments, and a more varied re-ordering of events for a desired effect.

In a true crime story the elements are constant, regardless of where or when: the recipe has a number of ingredients and in each case the choices facing the writer are about the benefits of each reshuffle. To make this plain, consider these options for openings:

The facts of the case: crime described; account of the victim and the place; who was at the crime scene first and why.

The dramatic effect: the actual crime is in focus, with as much particular description as you wish; of course this may include the imagined nature of the crime, as deduced from forensic evidence.

The result: there are advantages to telling the story at the end; this method is often favoured by writers who like to give the reader a reverse puzzle – a case how a man came to be sentenced to death. It often works well if the tale begins with the sentence, then retraces the story of the crime, and ends with jail or any other destination, from scaffold to asylum.

Whatever the chosen approach, the point is that there are only so many constituents with each genre of crime writing. If we look at some of the most popular here, it is possible to list these constituents.

The commonest narrative subjects are: gangland, large-scale white collar crime, scaffold stories, serial killers, mass murder and perversion. Each of these contains a number of spin-off subjects, so that 'perversion' includes anything from cannibalism to buggery. 'Gangland' could be anything from a city mob to a global mafia. Taking just one – the scaffold story – here are the established constituents:

The biography of the killer

The moral focus

The planning of the murder or other capital offence

The thrill of empathic fantasy

The investigation

The trial

Retribution

Even within these we could break down the elements, so that in the final stage, the retribution, of a scaffold story, we could have: death cell/ officers/ religious perspectives / mental state of the convict/ the hangman and his ritual/ media response. There may even be others, but this is a basic list, and this could be extended into the other popular stories.

Tutorial

We have looked at a few established approaches to true crime writing here; of course there is always scope for innovation, and that is an issue. This is because of the denigration of the genre in literary circles. A glance through the review pages of newspapers and periodicals will illustrate this. True crime, along with westerns, romance and science fiction, tends to be marginalised in the book pages. It is often thought that true crime writing lacks literary merit and is composed solely of pot-boilers, books responding to current crimes, rushed into print and written by hacks. It is often forgotten that true crime books are increasingly being rated on the lists of what is often called 'creative non-fiction.'

That is why this chapter has been about literary, stylistic choices: writing today has to push the boundaries as never before, so reflection on choices of the storytelling options is so crucially important.

The sense of place and atmosphere is always a key factor in the success of the writing in this genre. The varieties of this described above are, again, merely a starting-point. It should never be forgotten that in today's literary world of the fusion of all genres, there is always room for innovation.

****

5

THE CLASSIC NARRATIVE

One-minute summary

As already mentioned, there is a classic template of the true crime story, and that simply follows the established structure of life itself. If we think of the story as a string of beads then the three essential beads are crime-pursuit-retribution. Then we can add motivation – circumstances – escape – remorse –punishment. In modern writing all of these may have a psychological element too. So that 'remorse' may be written in all kinds of ways. To say that a person felt remorse is very different from a detailed account of the pain involved in that emotion. Imagine the remorse of a husband and father who has taken the life of his wife in a drunken rage. Compare that with the remorse of someone who meant to kill but has since changed fundamentally and has to create a new identity almost, to live again.

This chapter therefore deals with each of these key elements. Again, each element presents us with a number of choices: what to select and what to reject, and why. The best advice is that, whatever choices are made, motivation remains at the core. Why did the criminal do the act? That will be the focus always, and that question will be relevant in every stage of your story. The classic elements of a true crime story will always have new updates and several permutations depending on creative choices; but every choice has a consequence for the rest of the narrative of course, like placing a card in a house of cards.

The Crime

Let's start with a case study. Here is an account of a crime from recent times.

A Murderous Attack in Church 1948

Some cases of homicide are particularly complicated with the problem of finding out exactly what the circumstances are that led to a violent death. If we have a death in which two people struggled and grappled in extreme passion, with no-one else present, then everything in court is going to rest on exactly what went on and who did what. Today, with the modern sophisticated techniques of forensics applied to materials at the scene of crime, a detailed narrative of events leading to a death may be constructed with scientific support. But sixty years ago, when two women fought in a Dublin church, there was uncertainty as to exactly how the struggle resulted in a death.

The fight happened in the Glasnevin church of Our Lady of the Seven Dolours. The church has now been replaced by a more modern building so again, we have to imagine the scene and its physical environment, but what happened was that Mary Gibbons, who was eighty-three years old and lived in Botanic Avenue, walked to church in August, 1948, as she did every day. She walked through a warm summer day to the dark interior of the church and there she found a pew and began to pray. She was near the confessional, but was completely alone in the church – at least until the door opened again and someone else came in. The door closed after a beam of light had shot in momentarily.

Then we have another woman's story before we find out what happened in the church. Mary Daly was very hard up. Her landlady said that she was living at this time in lodgings with her husband and

54

child, in Botanic Road. They had a struggle to find the weekly rent. Mary had been to beg money from a priest, things were so bad, and he had given her the cash for the week's rent. But it was always going to be a constant battle to survive. In desperation, Mary went to the church in Glasnevin that day, but she had a hammer in her shopping-bag. Her motives will always be a mystery, but the fact is that she went to the church with that potential murder weapon.

As Mary Gibbons prayed she was suddenly aware of a crack on her head. She was a large woman, well-built and still with some strength in spite of her age. After an initial sense of sheer stunned shock she turned to find Mary Daly, who was small and lightly made, wielding a hammer in the light of the church candle. One second she had been saying her hail Marys and the next she was fighting for her life.

Mary grabbed Mary Daly's hand and the fight began. Mary Gibbons was bleeding profusely and she broke away and ran to the door of the church to cry for help but more hammer blows were slammed on her head. There was a trail of blood from the pew where the attack began, right to the door.

Some children came to church at that moment and they heard the cries and screams inside, so they decided to run for help and at last, two adults came to try to help. A local butcher called James Canavan and a lorry driver called Thomas Mitchell rushed to the church and they had to force open the door, as one woman was lodged against it. When they forced their way inside, Mitchell immediately realised he had to snatch the hammer from the smaller woman, and he did so, while Canavan tried to help the old lady in her pain. What happened then could have been the scene of any small-scale street brawl in Dublin – something not that uncommon. But it was the beginning of the confusion set before the forces of law in court, because a crowd had gathered, including the children, and what they saw and heard was not a hammer attack from behind but two women screaming, accusing each other of violence.

Old Mary Gibbons naturally told everyone that the younger woman had attacked her, but Daly then retorted with an accusation that Gibbons had tried to rob her and snatch her handbag. Detective Sergeant Joe Turner then arrived and that was the scene of noise and confusion he saw, and in a most unseemly place. An ambulance was called and Turner questioned Daly, who insisted that the old woman had tried to steal her bag. 'I was struggling with her to get my bag back!' she said.

As for Mary Gibbons, who was in hospital as Mary Daly was carried off to the police station, she was very seriously injured. Her skull had several wounds and bones were cracked; but she was able to give evidence in a special court held in the hospital of Mater Misericordiae in Eccles Street. It was to be a period of uncertainty for all concerned, mainly because the victim was confused about the actual events in the church. There was no confidence in her medical condition being either one thing or the other. At first, the doctors thought that she was pulling through and so when Daly stood before Judge O'Flynn on 16 August, the charge was wounding with intent, not attempted murder. But that was to change: at first the old lady was thought to be 'out of danger' but within a day she was dead. Back came Mary Daly to court to face a murder charge.

The trial was on 8 November at the Dublin Central Court. From the accused's home and family situation there came a motive, put together by the counsel for the prosecution, Sir John Esmonde. The financial difficulties of the Daly family (with a young baby to support) meant that facts were uncovered that showed how desperate Mary Daly would be to get hold of some money; there had been a court order served on her to pay her rent. It was in the Church of the Seven

Dolours that a priest had given her money just a short time before the attack, so it was an easy matter to find a motive in her return to that church in such dire straits. Was she carrying the hammer in case she had to extort money with threats this time, as opposed to begging and hoping for further largesse from the priest? That seemed to be the case.

The issue was, as there were no witnesses, whether or not Mary Daly went to the church with an intent to kill for money or whether there were other reasons for what she had in her bag that day. Testimony from the lorry driver who saw her that day and who restrained her, Mr Mitchell, was that Daly was distressed and excited, and that she did say that the hammer, which she had bought in Woolworth's store, was hers; similarly, the children in court, who heard the attack but did not see it, said that they did hear a voice saying 'Help... she's murdering me!' So who was doing the attacking?

Mary Daly was small and the older Mary Gibbons was tall and well-made; that was a factor that complicated things of course. Daly's defence argument was still that Gibbons had taken the hammer and attacked her; she may have been just five feet two tall and delicately made, but in the end, who had the clear motive? Why would the old lady have attacked Daly? The defence brought in a medical expert to say that the accused was so frail that she could not have used a hammer, and on the matter of her financial straits, Daly said that she did have five pounds on her that day, and that the old lady was intending to steal that from her. The lengthy defence narrative was the familiar one of self-defence, creating a story in which Dalty, going into the church for quiet prayer and carrying her bag and purse, was attacked in the semi-darkness and that she happened to have the hammer with her and so she used it. That does not sit easily with the statement that she was too delicate to use a hammer.

The contradictions and confusions continued as Daly claimed that she had only at first hit Gibbons on the arm, that the old lady took the hammer and turned on her; being the stronger, she argued, the old lady then set about whacking her about the body with the weapon. She said, 'I tried to get out the door. I could not as the woman was leaning against it. I kept shouting for my husband for help. I thought I heard footsteps outside. I gave the woman another blow of the hammer on the head.. I did not know where I was hitting her. I hit her to get rid of her.'

The defence really dramatised this situation with great emotional emphasis, saying, 'Anyone who found themselves in Mrs Daly's position would probably have acted as she had done. There was no criminal intent.' But the judge pointed out that Mrs Gibbons had been praying and so that small as she was, Daly would have approached the old lady from a position above. That was a hypothetical detail that had some influence on the jury, who were out to deliberate for an hour or so and came back in with a guilty verdict, though they recommended mercy. But the sentence was one of hanging, with a date fixed in December that year.

The final chapter of this case is one of an incredible series of appeals; a date for appeal was set and then everything depended on points of law, mainly that the deceased had made a formal 'dying declaration' regarding the attack (at that time only one of minor assault of course) and that such a matter could not be admissible in a murder trial. In an example of what must have been a desperately stressful situation, the judges rejected this but then opened up the possibility of a final appeal to the Supreme Court. There was then a complete re-trial because of legal technicalities, and again the judgement was guilty of murder. For a second time Mary Daly stood in court and heard her death sentence. But the string of frustrating and dramatic trials ended there, as shortly *after that second decision her sentence was commuted to life imprisonment. Mary did a seven-year stretch, followed by time with a religious order, and then went back into her life.*

Only very rarely in criminal trials has there been such doubt and uncertainty about the actual events of a case, and the fact that so many people arrived on the scene just a little too late to have any definite evidence on the series of events in the fight only served to make the trial more complex.

The key elements are the motivation- the opportunity-the place – the punishment. As it turned out the remission from the capital sentence was the most sensational aspect. There was doubt about many of the small incidences recalled in the church that day, and uncertainties about the intention to kill. Of course, the killer was a woman and there was a psychological profile. In other words, this was more complex than at first met the eye. It cries out for more information – particularly as we learn that she went to 'a religious order.'

The crime may be major or simply an everyday thing, but the consequences, and in fact the character involved and the community, add layers of interest. But of course there is a hierarchy and at the top are murder and treason, perhaps along with high-level robbery such as the Great Train Robbery. Murder is and always has been the generic heart of true crime, based as it is on the planned taking of a human life. Its borderline with manslaughter, and also the courtroom defences over the centuries, present infinite possibilities for creative writing.

There is also the question of the inherent interest in the crime as a resolution of a moral dilemma. Where the moral and criminal issues have a total eclipse is where the most intriguing crime stories lie. But perhaps most baffling of all are the crime stories in which all explicable human behaviour falls short of offering explanation, and so we have the borderline with madness.

In most of my ten regional casebooks, I have written about serious crime and insanity as adjoining states in the geography of homicide. In the nineteenth century, as adversarial trials began to be established, and before the accused could speak in court (which happened in the 1890s) the defences of provocation and insanity took centre stage. The records have hundreds of homicides in which a husband shot or stabbed his wife while he was intoxicated. Time and again, drunkenness as a form of temporary insanity was put forward as a defence, and almost always it failed to prevent a hanging or a sentence for life in Broadmoor. The point at which the moral and criminal issues meet often tends to be found in such crimes – they go against the bonds of working class community in the time period referred to.

The Pursuit
What could be more exciting than an account of the police in search of 'their man?' The idea of a pursuit of a wanted man leads into the dark centuries of outlawry in England, and also to the Wild West and its bounty hunters and sheriffs. In Britain, the advent of the professional detective force in 1842 really established the notion of a pursuit as a key element in true crime. Before the mid-Victorian years of course there had been constables and Bow Street Runners, and London police had gone out into the provinces to help in the fight against Chartists and Luddites in the Regency period, but it was the professional detective who brought about a more complex aspect of pursuit. Nevertheless, the hunted man, the man on the run, presents one of the most dramatic episodes in the genre. Whether it is Harry Roberts, the man who killed two police officers in 1966 and then went literally 'underground' or whether it is George Bidwell, one of the American gang who brought

off a massive fraud on the Bank of England in 1877 and went on the run, the excitement of the chase is at the heart of things.

Often, the hunt, along with changes of identity, disguise and trickery, make the aspects of the genre in which there is the closest boundary with crime fiction. Guidelines for writing this might be put like this:

Stretch the episodes on the run to bring in new scenes and people
Use the pursuit to develop character – of villains and pursuers
Use techniques such as filmic, episodic writing to add drama to this.

The Arrest and Trial

It goes without saying that as an arrest takes place, there is drama. A classic example – one combining pursuit with arrest, is the story of Dr Crippen.

Crippen, an American with interests in fringe medicine and dentistry, settled with his wife, musical artiste Belle Elmore, in North London in 1900. Their address has become one of the most notorious in the History of murder: 39, Hilldrop Crescent. They had a strange, unconventional life; Belle was a member of the music hall and variety fraternity but had very little work; she took in paying guests to make ends meet. Crippen became very friendly with a secretary, Ethel Le Neve, and after spending time together with little thought for what people might think, it became obvious to many in their circle that Ethel was not at home – or anywhere else. Crippen concocted a fabrication that she had returned to America because her mother had died, and then later he broke the news that Belle herself was dead. But eventually her worried friends, with plenty of cause for suspicion, went to tell the police about Belle's disappearance.

The man who took charge of the investigation was Walter Dew. He was from Northamptonshire, and was forty-seven at that time; he had been in the Metropolitan Police for thirty years and had been part of the group of detectives working on the Jack the Ripper case. When the Crippen case came along, he came to realise the importance of it, and how it would engage the public imagination. He sat and listened to the story told by John Nash and Lil Hawthorne, two of Belle's closest friends, and then he went, together with Sergeant Arthur Mitchell, to pay a call on Crippen.

Belle had indeed been murdered; Crippen had shot her and buried her under the floor of the cellar. The Crippens had a French servant, and she opened the door to Dew. It was to be a visit that would cause recriminations aimed at Dew later on. Ethel Le Neve was in the house: a point that was of utmost significance of course. Crippen was at work, at his business address and Dew insisted that Ethel went with them to that address. Dew's words when he came face to face with Crippen are loaded with irony to this day: 'I am Inspector Dew and this is Sergeant Mitchell, of Scotland Yard. Some of your wife's friends have been to us concerning the stories you have told them about her death, with which they are not satisfied. I have made exhaustive enquiries and I am not satisfied so I have come here to see you to ask if you care to offer any explanation.'

Dew was a very experienced policeman. He was being careful; so cautious was he that he began to take a very long statement and soon the two men were delving deeply into Crippen's life. It was then that a truly unusual step was taken: that the detective and Crippen should have lunch together. As they sat in an Italian restaurant in Holborn, naturally Dew was studying his suspect. But Crippen ate heartily and appeared to be free from any nervous anxieties or defensive manoeuvres in the conversation. All that encouraged Dew to take an open-minded view of matters.

It was late in the afternoon before attention switched to Ethel. Her story, told repeatedly after the terrible events of the murder and the aftermath, was that she was deceived by Crippen. Dew had come up against a criminal who was capable of misleading anyone, as he presented to the world an eccentric mix of professionalism and bluster. But when Crippen and Ethel were on the run, going to Holland and then with the intention of traveling from there to America, Dew went with his sergeant back to Hilldrop Crescent and then the discovery of Belle's body was made. This time, the search was a thorough one; first they found a pistol in a cupboard and a sheet of paper with Belle's signature written on it.

After that it was only a matter of time before they reached the cellar and on 13 July 1910 Dew picked up a poker, tested the bricks on the floor, and the end of the poker went between two bricks. Then it was a case of going down there. Dew wrote later, 'Presently a little thrill went through me... I then produced a spade from the garden and dug the clay that was immediately beneath the bricks. After digging down to a depth of about four spadefuls I came across what appeared to be human remains.' It was big business for the Yard. The Assistant Commissioner came to the scene, MacNaghten, who had the presence of mind to take cigars with him, to help cope with the noxious fumes that Dew had said were emanating from the remains.

One remarkable aspect of this dig in the cellar was the way in which the scene of crime was not 'safe' in terms of forensic methodology. Disinfectant was used, for instance, and therefore all kinds of substances were removed which may well have been important later. Of course the hunt for the fugitives was then in process.

In the annals of detection the Crippen case is, of course, celebrated as being the first time that the telegraph was used to help capture a murderer. But the 'detective work' was actually done by the

Commander of the ship that Crippen and Ethel were on, the Montrose. This was Henry Kendall, and he was very observant. Ethel was traveling in the clothes of a young man, and for most of the time that seems to have been effective; but Kendall had slight suspicions when he saw the clothes and noted that her movements were not masculine. Finally, he saw Ethel squeezing Crippen's hand and that was the detail that led to his certainty that here he had the fugitives on his ship.

The wireless telegraph was then used, somewhat momentously; the submarine cable had been used sixteen years earlier, to catch a murderer called Muller who was also on board ship heading for America. Another killer, named Tawell, had been spotted on a train and the telegraph was used to make sure that police were waiting for him as he alighted. But now the wireless telegraph was used and a dramatic pursuit on a faster ship meant that Dew was waiting for Crippen when he docked.

The elements of the case are well known, but the most interesting aspect of the arrest and the following events are in the relationship of the media with the detectives involved. Dew made enemies, as he did not co-operate. He was, naturally, the subject of a media frenzy and was offered large amounts of money for his story. So high profile was the case that, as the build-up to the trial proceeded, the Pinkerton agency were brought in, their task being to protect key witnesses who had to journey over the Atlantic to London. Criticisms of Dew's handling of the whole affair, right from the start, now began. Even the famous judge, Sir Travers Humphreys, joined in with the criticism, as in the fact that Belle's furs were still at Hilldrop Crescent – an oversight on Dew's part at the time of his first inspection there. The essence of that line of thought was the rhetorical question: what woman would go to America for a lengthy stay and not take her furs?

The element of the trial that is often overlooked is the actual physical nature of the place. A crime writer needs to spend time in a

Victorian or Edwardian courthouse. There is no substitute for knowing that actual place where men stood in the dock and judges sat in judgment. I visited the current criminal court in Dublin not long ago, and not only did I see all that shiny wood and the different levels at which people would be seated: I also visited the cells beneath. The experience gave me the best insight I have ever had into the experiences of some of the men and women I had written about.

The court itself is ritualistic of course, and any kind of ritual, of professional distancing from plain reality, invites reflection on class and status, and on the deepest nature of authority in British history. Therefore, the episode concerning trials in the true crime book should maximize the opportunity for reflecting and explaining for the reader how the reality of a courtroom relates to the criminal justice system itself – as a concept, as a mechanism for authority, and as visible judgment by the state on transgressors. One of the very best sources for researching this is in the series known as Notable British Trials (see bibliography) published by William Hodge. These volumes provide information on the whole course of the trials of infamous criminals: they also present verbatim accounts given, as in this, a statement by P C Beanland, who was stationed at Old Trafford in the 1870s when the great killer and thief Charles Peace was on the rampage. He gives an account of finding the police officer who was killed by Peace, a man called Cock: ' I ran with all my might to West Point and found a great confusion... men trying to stop the horses in the carts... I found Cock with his head against the wall, and his feet on a small flag. He was bruised on the temple and the cheek bone....'

Closure

Think about the finality of the classic crime story: of all the popular genres, true crime surely has a claim to have the most stunning repertoire of horrible, fateful finality in its writing: the Regency narrative of the scaffold has this in its barest form: a long and powerful account of the last hours of the condemned person, together with the effort to repent or feel remorse and the final moments on the scaffold with the noose ready to be tightened around the neck- this is closure.

But even a strong murder story may not end with execution or even life imprisonment of course. It may lead to the asylum and 'Her Majesty's Pleasure.' Of course, there is a counter argument in murder tales and stories of other serious crime: the inner emotional and spiritual turmoil of the criminal imprisoned for life. In my experience, after working in prisons for six years, the general public have no real understanding of the nature of being in a cell, with no prospect of release, or even the experience of a prison cell with a release date known. The point is that your freedom has been taken away. There is no possibility of taking a walk to the corner shop or going to walk the dog in the park on a lovely summer day. No, there are high walls, gates with locks and a general air of depression. Days drag. As the poet Milton once wrote 'Oh aching time, oh moments big as years!' That would be the defining poetic line about incarceration.

This classic crime narrative closure is being stressed here because it is always an option. You might find more innovative ones, but the reader always enjoys the urge to reflect yet again on the truly awesome thought of a violent and judicial killing or the prospect of never seeing normal life 'outside' again.

Of course, the closure of the story is not necessarily an 'ending' and that word is somewhat outmoded and too simple now, when stories are very sophisticated and reading no longer an innocent pleasure for many of us. This means that a closure in true crime may be a simple suggestion that a person's real punishment is going to be unavoidable, even in normal life. There are also the resources of the shifting point of view. Point of view (POV) opens up so many possibilities. In its simplest forms, it can offer the viewpoints of the victim, the offender, the bystander, the memoirist, an omniscient narrator and many more.

A lot depends, in a true crime closure, on whether you select an opening, uplifting closure or a hugely powerful dark one. These two closures of stories from a crime casebook show some interesting contrasts:

(a)

Barnetby, a small place where not much happens, was not exactly a village with a peaceful image at the time; not long after this, a young woman pulled up on a bike and walked into a post office, threatening to shoot someone. In the decade or so after the end of the war, its position 'on the road' where people might stop for petrol or refreshments, might have been good for local trade, but the other side of that was a dark one – it was a place where men like Smith would be tempted to stop (or forced to top) and mayhem might follow. On this occasion, the right man for the job was on the spot, cool, calm and brave. A quiet, dependable local man had done things 'beyond the call of duty' that day, which started with the routine of every other day, and ended like a car-chase scene from Hollywood.

(b)

We can only imagine the reactions of the accused as they stood so long in the dock, desperately trying to follow the arguments of the learned men in robes, with the asthmatic Maule coughing through the whole proceedings. But it was not a happy outcome for them. That particular bench wanted to set an example. It was just another street robbery, but this time it went to the Crown Court; the gang of rough miscreants must have been shuddering in their boots. They had picked on the wrong type of victim this time. Worse still for them: they had no lawyer for them with any notable degree of smartness or 'gift of the gab' when the odds were against them.

The context for all this street violence was one of extreme deprivation. *The Times* reported in 1847 that in Manchester, 'The streets are crowded with paupers, most of them Irish, who have travelled to Manchester from Liverpool.. in hope of obtaining... the public bounty of the town. A soup kitchen has been established...' and in his novel of 1847, partly set in Liverpool, Herman Melville wrote: ' of all the sea-ports in the world, Liverpool abounds in all the variety of land-sharks, land-rats, and other vermin which make the hapless mariner their prey.' (From *Redburn*)

These are both accounts of twentieth century robberies. Both are written to raise the spirits: that is, justice has been done and there has been in (a) an ordinary act of heroism and in (b) tough justice in court. Notice how the second uses wider reference and uses a quote for a literary work; this makes a contrast, but also, there is the basic similarity of a certain level or purposely easygoing and low key vocabulary to bring down the story, away from the easy rhetoric of the classic closure of terror, hard punishment or violence.

Tutorial

This chapter has been about options. All creative writing is a case of coping with options at all stages. We have looked at the template for those true crime stories that deal with a historical perspective or with the simple, direct ways in which law and community relate to serious crime. This has also meant that we considered the taut, often brutal and gory option of the bloody state vengeance involved in the classic story.

Finally, the main food for thought here has to be about whether or not to write close, like a camera always in close-up, or to open out to something more like a long-shot, or even panoramic.

6

WRITING A CASE BOOK

One-Minute Summary
Of all the sub-genres of true crime and crime history, the case- book remains a constant on the publishing scene: an evergreen that takes various forms. The basic idea is that the book comprises a number of chapters either covering a variety of crime stories from one locale, or stories clustering around a theme. As I write this, one publishing house, Amberley, has just begun a series called Murders and Misdemeanours: the series has local, regional material, and the crimes are mixed, though murder takes centre-stage.

A casebook may be organised in various ways:

A chronological sequence
Clearly, this is well established and readers like the simplicity. The main advantage of this is that the spin-off material from the backbone stories provide a commentary on the development of crime and on legislation in relation to society and politics.

Arrangement by Crime
It also makes sense to group the stories around specific offences, so that you might use terms such as 'Homicide' (so material can include cases of murder, manslaughter, suicide etc.); and then 'Fraud and Deception' or 'Slander and Libel' and so on. This enables you to open up a grouping of similar crimes, and again these might span centuries and so interesting contrasts may be made.

Biographical Focus

The clusters of stories may be done around individuals, so that such sections as 'Killers' or 'Detectives' might be used.

Contrastive Tales

There is also scope for grouping the sections in the book by the nature of the cases. You might have a number of quite comic tales – inept criminals. Or there may be several in which the same lawyers/judges are involved. Another approach might be to put the focus on the forensics of each case and put these aspects into prominence.

Choices and Balance

In order to make the subject of selection and rejection for a case book clear, here is an example of a contents page. It is from my book, *Foul Deeds and Suspicious Deaths in Liverpool* (see bibliography).

Contents

Several things should strike one as important here. First, the chapter headings. Notice how the aim is to provide a dramatic or intriguing title if possible. But even this is varied, so that 'The McKenzie Murder Case' – a plain and direct heading – is put alongside 'A Man Beset by Demons.' In other words, even the chapter headings suggest the variety.

To have everything suggesting a dynamic and sensational treatment of the subject might put the reader off, thinking the stories were all overwritten for effect.

But also, note that some headings hint at the crime, such as the word 'stash' in chapter 34, while others leave options open. Even 'The Wallace Mystery' (a murder case) is not defined in the title. In fact, the crimes covered include poaching, poisoning, domestic violence, gang attacks, riots and fraud, to name just a selection. In the end, variety is the secret.

The choice of material and the balance aimed at should, naturally, relate to the place if the theme is regional. Liverpool is a great port so the reader would expect some tales related to that industry. In my books on the cities and towns of the West Riding conurbations, I knew that the emphasis had to be on urban, domestic and trade crime. The plain fact is that the new towns of the Industrial Revolution had overcrowding, unemployment, mass illness, public disorder and industrial strife. The selection process reflected this fact.

Drama and Fact

I would like to illustrate this with reference to an extract from a short true crime story.

In the 'Ripper year' of 1888, there was a flood of hoax letters to the police. Clearly, such hoaxes are a very stupid and dangerous activity. The culprits are very difficult to track down, but Bradford appears to be the only place in which a writer of such a letter was caught and charged. She was Maria Coroner, a Canadian-born milliner living in Westgrove Street, a woman with a dark side. She had written to the local newspaper and to the Chief Constable, saying when caught that she had done it as a joke, and the whole affair attracted a large media interest when she appeared in court on 23 October that year.

Maria was fined £20 and bound over to keep the peace for six months. One newspaper report said that 'a dense crowd fought for admission to the court.' It has disturbing echoes of Wearside Jack and the Yorkshire Ripper hoax in our own time. But in an age when the popular press made great sensational tales out of commonplace domestic killings, the strange twisted fantasy that produces 'Ripper letters' can to a certain extent be understood.

The Maria Coroner case is a curiosity, but we can add to that something far more startling and intriguing that happened in Bradford that year – it may have been the Ripper himself who came north to kill, and perhaps after taunting the metropolitan Police with his own terrible letters. This is the extract:

Just after Christmas, 1888, John Gill of Thorncliff Road, went for a ride on a milk cart. It was very early in the morning, and his mother never saw him alive again. He had been seen playing but also, menacingly, he was seen talking to a man, a stranger to the area by all accounts. The family soon felt the distress of his absence, and feared the worst; they placed a poster on view, with a physical description of him, and actually used the word 'lost' despite the fact that it was only a day after his disappearance.

John, eight years old, was found in a stable by Joe Buckle, a butcher. Joe was cleaning the place when he saw a pile of some indescribable object, and looking closer, he saw that it was a corpse, and most noticeable on first inspection was the fact that one ear had been sliced off. He ran for help. Later, when a closer inspection was made by officers, it was found that there had been extreme mutilation of the body; his stomach had been cut open and vital organs place don top of him. He had been repeatedly cut, stabbed in the chest, and there was a rough noose around his neck.

This is where the complex business of the massive number of Ripper letters figure in the story. The pathology certainly makes the Gill murder a contender for being classified as a Ripper killing; Dr Bond in London, when writing about the body of victim Mary Kelly, noted that 'the viscera were found in various parts... the liver between the feet and the spleen by the left side of the body.' There are similarities, but the main argument for the Ripper coming north rests on the statements made in the letters. As Philip Sugden has written, 'The important question is... whether any of these letters we have noticed was written by the murderer.' This was said about the first letter received, well before the Bradford case. By the time of the Gill killing, police were walking into Whitechapel in pairs and detectives were everywhere around the area. Five killings had taken place in London, the last in November, just a month before the Bradford case.

At the end of November, one of the Ripper letters had the text, 'I shall do another murder on some young youth such as printing lads who work in the city. I did write you once before... I shall do them worse than the women, I shall take their hearts...' The crime writer, Patricia Cornwell, believes that the Bradford murder is worth serious consideration. But the problem with Patricia Cornwell's use of the Ripper letters in associating the Bradford case with Jack is that she talks of the 'Ripper letter' as if their provenance is certified and that certain examples cluster together as the work of individual authors (see her book, Portrait of a Killer). This is why she dismisses the most tantalising scrap of detail in poor John Gill's murder: that a piece of a Liverpool newspaper was used to wrap part of the body. Even more fascinating, the paper had a name on it: 'W Mason, Derby Road.'

Those ripperologists who think that the mystery killer was James Maybrick, merchant of Liverpool, would perhaps point to the fact that Maybrick was most probably meeting someone in Manchester at one point in 1888, but otherwise, apparently never went near Bradford. Recent writing on Maybrick, and notably the new work done by handwriting and paper experts on the celebrated book, *The Diaries of Jack the Ripper* would seem to confirm that there is no factual evidence for the Bradford connection. We have known for a long time that there was a Lancashire connection, because of James Bierley from Rochdale, who was linked to the Maybrick family.

The Ripper letters in the hand of the painter Walter Sickert, whom Cornwell believes to have been the Ripper, also contain one text that reads, 'I riped[sic] up a little boy in Bradford.' The great Sherlock Holmes would have reacted to this by insisting that, though these Bradford letters may have been by the same hand, there is nothing to prove that they belonged to the man we know as Jack the Ripper. In other words, what we most likely have here is that well-known phenomenon in homicide, the copycat crime.

Bradford was, as Patricia Cornwell points out, a city on the tour being made by the great actor Sir Henry Irving, and Sickert had also been an actor, and was fond of playgoing. If he had gone north to distract affairs from Whitechapel, as Cornwell points out, 'Many of the cities mentioned in the Ripper letters were on Henry Irving's theatre company's schedule, which was published in the newspapers daily...' The same is said in her book about race courses, another passion of Sickert's, and of course, it is not difficult to find race courses near Bradford in 1888. This is all speculation, but interesting nevertheless.

The existence of the Bradford references open up new possibilities, but beneath all the hype and speculation, we have the existence of such copycat crimes and the psychology of serial killing now very much established in academic study. The thought behind killer profiling does not find satisfactory lines of thought in the Gill murder. It is not convincing that the sexual-sadistic Ripper would switch to murders of *young men, and also the use of the noose is bizarre as a scene of crime ritual communication, as such killers tend to do. Another curious detail on Gill's body was a piece of torn shirting about his neck – again, hardly a signature of the Ripper in London.*

As far as the Bradford connection is concerned, the events could have turned out tragically for the prime local suspect, one Bill Barrett, the a dairyman, but he was cleared and had had 'a long interview' with his legal adviser that was undoubtedly the basis of a sound defence. The only evidence was circumstantial. If the killing was a copycat murder, then the identity of the real killer remains a mystery, and the Gill case is in the annals of unsolved crimes.

The Bradford case is not the only one that may be another Ripper victim outside Whitechapel. In June, 1887, at Temple Stairs on the Thames, parts of a body previously found at Rainham were found in a parcel. At the inquest it was asserted that someone with a knowledge of anatomy had done this ghastly murder. Eventually, as in this Bradford scenario, a letter supposedly from the 'real' Ripper denied any involvement with these body parts. At least the Bradford killing had some definite pointers to the actual Ripper.

From the very beginning of the research for this story, I was faced with the undeniable evidence that the source was all theoretical. There may never have been anything more in the Bradford crime than a copycat murder. But this extract illustrates the need to stretch the material to its limits if the theory or supposition allows. In other words, there is a certain possibility that the Bradford killing was Jack, and no less a writer than Patricia Cornwell has gone into this before, also linking Sickert to the case. Your task as a writer coming after this first material is to raise questions and summarise theories. That has to be mixed with the drama inherent in the story.

That is the reason for drama and fact to be well conjoined and written into a seamless narrative.

Some Examples

Casebooks often present examples that have a certain dullness, because the writer has gone on doggedly with limited material. This is where the sources come back again into usefulness. The case book story has these categories of ingredients:

The story itself, as first reported
The legal process
The social context – with its contemporary vocabulary and reference.
Other primary sources

n each of these extracts from true crime books (all mine) locate each of these elements and note how they intermix:

(a)

In the language of crime, uttering does not mean speaking: it refers to the crime of forgery, a very serious offence which until the 1820's in England was punishable by death. In 1853 one of the more bizarre examples of this criminality took place, and the culprit was a vicar, the Rev. Beresford. He forged an endorsement of a bill for the sum of £100 – a great deal of money at the time. The case was sensational locally because he was a clergyman but also 'highly connected, and next heir to a peerage.'

In October, 1849, Beresford called at the offices of the Bradford Banking Company and asked the manager to discount a bill from a London company called Hibbert. The practice then was for a bill like that to be signed and endorsed by a prominent person, so Beresford asked if such a signature from Mr Kay of Manningham Hall would be acceptable and was told it would be. What happened next was strange indeed.

A letter arrived at the bank, addressed to Beresford, and the clergyman arrived to collect it, opened it, and then presented it for discount. It had a signature purporting to be by Kay. The manager was suspicious as he was not convinced that the endorsement was genuine. There was the signature – John Cunliffe Kay. At that point, Beresford's conman skills came into play as he managed to persuade the manager that Kay had been ill when visited and would have had a shaky hand. The manager was impressed and discounted the bill.

Actually, Kay had been approached by Beresford but had refused to sign. Beresford then forged the signature, taking it from a letter written some time before. But fate was against the forger; he was not traced by any police work or by a smart detective. Kay accidentally met him walking in Regent Street and had him arrested. Kay, as a witness, recalled Beresford visiting the Hall. What emerged was that some time before, the vicar had been introduced to Kay by his mother-in-law, as a relative of hers. It was noted in court that the accused 'Was a cousin of Lord Decies, and next heir to the peerage. He told Kay that he would be Lord Decies in the spring, that he was married and had a daughter of fifteen years of age.

The counsel for the defence ran through half a dozen reasons why the prosecution was foolish and misguided, by Baron Martin, the judge, dismissed them all, insisting that the only points of interest were whether Beresford knowingly forged the signature and whether the endorsement was forged. The jury found Beresford guilty and he was sentenced to transportation for the period of his natural life. A report at the time was: 'On hearing the sentence, the prisoner seemed astounded; he staggered, and was removed from the dock supported by the officers.

It was rumoured in court that he had a living in Cork of £1,000 a year, which has been sequestered for his debts. '
Heroes, Villains and Victims of Bradford

(b)

Edward Hall liked a drink. In fact he liked to have an enormous quantity of drink, and that always led him into trouble. In July, 1831, it led him to the gallows in Lincoln.

Hall, just twenty-two, was out filling himself with beer one June evening in Grimsby and he made too much noise for Edward Button, living near the alehouses where hall had a good time. Hall was making a nuisance of himself in a pub run by a Mr Kempsley and Button came to help the landlord throw the drunkard out into the street. After Hall was turfed out, Button still kept on his case, shouting through a window, 'Take him to the gaol, the rascal deserves to go for making such a row on a Sunday night.' Button was being a good citizen, expressing his moral views openly. The problem was that Hall felt anger and he vowed revenge.

'I'll kill Kempsley and somebody else!' he roared as he sharpened a knife on a stone a few days later. A witness heard him make that awful oath. A man called Milner, who spent time with hall, monitored the progress of the man's rankling hatred of the landlord and of Button.

Nothing much happened for a few days but on 2 July, Milner went out drinking with a man called Joseph Nash and also with Edward Button. They went along to the *Duke of York*, run by a Mrs Dines, and much later on, near midnight, Hall and his friend Ratton came in; Hall was in a raucous mood. Hall was out to provoke Button and he succeeded. The talk went like this, according to a witness: Button said, 'Hello! What do you want?'

'One bully has as much right here as another,' Hall answered, and Button followed that with a blow to Hall's face. Milner said that at first Button never even moved from his chair, but soon after there was a direct confrontation. Hall strode across to the far corner of the inn and challenged his enemy. 'I'm ready for you any time!'

A Lincoln pamphlet on the event reports the fight as being a desperate affair: 'In a short time both parties fell to the floor; they fell in the doorway leading from one room into another, there was no light in the other room, but it was not very dark where they fell...' What happened next must be a familiar tale from many a drunken brawl: one of the men had a knife, and of course, it was Hall. From the struggle on the floor, Button emerged, staggering into the light for all to see; then he managed to walk to a chair and there he sat down, clearly in great pain and bleeding. Someone at the scene said that he ground his teeth together and then died instantly.

A man opened Button's waistcoat because the crowd thought he was having a fit, but then the blood was evident and the man 'saw a wound on the fellow's breast.' The landlady screamed out loud that a man had been stabbed. As for Hall, in his drink he still had the wit to try to throw away the weapon; he appears to have gone outside to do that and then go back inside the inn where someone accused him. 'Hall, you have stabbed this man with a knife.' Hall said he had no knife on him.

Naturally, everyone there knew that he had been outside to throw away the murder weapon. Later in court, the daughter of the landlady said that she heard Hall provoke Button, saying, 'Come on!' She said he had one arm behind him – that was where he held the knife. She said that she followed the fight, holding a candle, and she said that she saw Hall holding Button fast to the ground, with a knee on him, and then the killer knocked away her candle. Before the light was out, though, she said, 'I saw a knife in Hall's hand.' She was not the only one there who saw that.

Evidence from the local surgeon confirmed that Button had suffered a deep two-inch long wound by his sternum and the knife 'had passed through the integuments in an oblique direction, upwards and inwards, entering between the fifth and sixth ribs. The doctor stated that there was no doubt that the knife-wound had caused the death of the deceased. In court, all this was heard in silence by the man in the dock, and he had nothing to say before a guilty verdict was passed on him.

The reporter in court noted that, ' The prisoner, during the whole of the trial, preserved a remarkable indifference to his fate, but afterwards he manifested a very different spirit.' That was after the judge donned the black cap and sentenced Hall to hang. The judge commented on 'the premeditated malice in the prisoner's mind, in having, on two separate occasions, sharpened a knife with a cool and deliberate intent to use such a weapon against one, if not two persons...' The reporter went on, saying that Hall's behaviour was then 'truly becoming, neither displaying excess of timidity nor unbecoming confidence, but looked forward to his approaching fate with calmness and resignation.' The assembled crowd by the tower at Cobb Hall, Lincoln Castle, had what they thought was good entertainment, many paying for the best views of the hanging from the inns across the road. They even enjoyed a long sermon on the sins of the condemned man. This was on 22 July 1831, and Hall must have wished he could have had more than the traditional final drink of ale at The Struggler public house by the castle walls.

Hanged at Lincoln

The hallmark was there at the scene, though it was not perceived at the time: Lily Waterhouse was fully dressed – apart from her boots.

There had been a violent struggle and the old lady had fought with some tenacity, as she was badly bruised, and it had taken several heavy blows to finish her. It is somewhat difficult to accept, bearing in mind the physical stature of Louie, that Lily Waterhouse had also been strangled. The killer, the police noticed, had cut up cloth to use to tie hands and feet; yet there must have been something else used to strangle the woman as the ligature marks on her neck were wider than that caused by a strip of cloth. It is a gruesome thought that the noises heard by the neighbours were almost certainly the movements of the dying woman's limbs as she was shaking in her death-throes. Her murderous lodger, small though she was, had been binding her tight, in an effort to stop the noises made by her feet; neighbours would certainly have heard the sounds, and would have come to ask questions. One important detail here is that the room was not carpeted. The sounds of feet thrashing on wooden boards could surely have meant that the murderer would have been disturbed as people responded to the noises heard through paper-thin walls.

What previously has read as the image of a widow leading a lonely and rather impoverished lifestyle, as questions were asked in the ensuing investigation, turned out to be something very different. In fact, some of Lily's previous lodgers hade been ladies of the night; these were tough times in Leeds and there was high unemployment. A widow with a low income would no doubt have been tempted to take in guests who would pay well, and no questions would be asked. But Lily was also unusual in that she had not been the isolated figure one might suppose. She had, since her husband's death, had lots of visitors and had lived quite an interesting life, including some dabbling in spiritualism. Neighbours, answering questions about her character, seemed eager to mention the shadier side of Lily's life, even to the point of one commenting that 'She was not a clean woman.' Understandably, these comments and implications about the victim led to the police trying to look for suspects among the clientele she had mixed with in the recent past.

Yorkshire's Murderous Women

In each of these I tried to achieve the various kinds of judicious balancing of material so that all four categories of subjects are there in some way.

Tutorial

The enjoyment of writing a casebook is rich indeed: it is the result of a long and fascinating process that tends to follow this pattern:

The research process

This is where all the material is gathered. The sources of this may be diverse and random. My practice is to gather everything relevant to each case in a folder for the chapter. These may then be knitted together in the writing.

The ordering of material

This is the point at which some of the files and documents will be rejected. The reasons for this are usually that a story is not complete and research has not made material available that would provide a satisfying closure for the reader. But at this stage the sequence of presentation needs to be worked out, along with the right chapter headings.

The Writing Itself

Whether one writes straight onto the screen or works methodically with a pen draft, the art here is to perhaps write everything down in a mess and then rewrite and edit, adding where necessary. Quotations are usually needed also, so at the research stage, all sources need to have been noted.

Factual Material

One infuriating tendency for many true crime books is that they often have no index of bibliography. This all depends on the publisher of course, but my advice is always to have these where necessary:

A bibliography listing primary and secondary sources

Appendices for important material – such as a glossary of terms or a dateline.

An index with names and main subjects.

****

7

WRITING FOR MAGAZINES

One-Minute Summary

Writing about real crime for magazines and periodicals tends to split into certain categories, as crime itself, in all its manifestations, percolates into a number of different markets and readerships. For instance, a crime writer with a background in law will have different interests to those of a writer with criminology interests. In terms of the people who write 'true crime' in its broadest expression, the interests and qualifications they have might range from history to sociology and from forensic science to psychology. But many true crime writers will cope with the elements of a story across the whole spectrum of these subjects, of course. It is a genre that lends itself to amateurism, but that does not necessarily equate with shoddy work. Far from it – some of the best true crime writers have no specific academic background but they have absorbed the essential factual basis for work as they have read and learned. Examples of the latter are Colin Wilson, Steve Fielding and Donald Thomas. To show the importance of informed amateurs in this genre, a look at crime features in daily newspapers is recommended: usually a successful blend of opinion, stunning fact and a dramatic tale.

Markets

With this in mind, the potential markets break down to this (in both Britain and in the USA):

The sensational popular monthlies

The True Crime Library publishes four of these, with additional summer and winter special issues; emphasis is given to crimes of violence and homicide, execution and various kinds of extreme deviance. The publications are *True Crime, Master Detective, Murder Most Foul* and *True Detective*. The writing treatments required are mainly extreme accounts of gore and guts; the readers enjoy the vicarious pleasure of the suffering of victims and of course of the criminals at the closure of the tale. The headlines say it all. Typical examples in recent issues have been 'A Good Flogging-Should Britain bring Back the Birch?' ; 'The 29 Hanged in Ireland'; 'Why Mary Shot the Preacher' and 'I Stabbed my Husband to Death.'

The kinds of words commonly used are such terms as shocker, mystery, rampage, horror and killing. The demand is for overwritten stories stretching the facts to extremes, but to be fair, these publications also engage in debate that tackles subjects of current importance, particularly when they run features on the criminal justice systems of other countries and take an international stance.

The serious journals

Because criminology reaches so far into a range of subjects – even war crimes or the Wild West - the monthly journals or more serious periodicals come into the freelancer's domain. For instance, the writer might choose a topic and then consider which of the following outlets would be most suitable: an historical magazine, a sociological or political journal, or an educational work. To clarify this, take the example of an issue of *History Today* in 2008, which carried a substantial article on the 1860 garotting crime wave in Victorian Britain. That publication is a serious historical magazine, intended for readers who want information in depth, written by experts and specialists. It would not be possible to 'mug up' on a subject and then write such a piece.

There is also the more social commentary variety of writing, dealing with a range of topics from prisons to police work, and from the jury system to miscarriages of justice. The point here is that the treatment needed is one that will highlight the issues and debates from an informed, strongly expressed position. Again, the place of the freelance amateur is fragile in this context. But that is not to say that there are no opportunities.

Educational

It should not be forgotten that there are plenty of general readers who like to learn more about crime and law than they may easily encounter in the papers. From school and college publications up to publications meant for the 'educated general reader' there are true crime topics waiting for the right approach and the right styles of narrative.

For example, the subject of current issues often opens up the importance of an historical perspective. A classic template for this category is the meeting of a current 'hot' topic with a centenary or anniversary. In 2007, there was the occasion of the centenary of the formal establishment of the probation service after the 1907 Probation of Offenders Act. Clearly, this was a topic linking to the always interesting subject of the rehabilitation of offenders and an historical landmark.

When such an occasion presents itself, then obviously, the opening is there to remind readers of some fundamental facts they may not know. This is an example of such a topic, part of an article relating a Victorian case to the notion of juvenile crime today:

This is a story about a very nasty child who almost killed two other children. It is not Dickens' Artful Dodger, and there is no loveable rogue in this Doncaster tale which shocked the local community and made the legal professionals think very carefully about the punishment required. It was an age without the notion of ASBO's.

In March 1866, Frederick Mason, just ten years old, was roaming around looking for mischief. He decided to entice two younger children away from their home in Rossington and put them through a terrible ordeal. He walked with them for a long time, so that he was nowhere near any other people, and then he began to beat them. He took a stick and struck them on the head and face; his victims were just five years and three years old, the eldest being a boy and the young one a girl.

After attacking them and seeming to enjoy their screams, he then took hold of them and threw them into the River Torne. Mason's behaviour defies explanation, particularly as he next sat on the bank eating some bread and meat and watched their struggles, then unbelievably, responding to their screams and cries for help, he swore at them and then dragged them out so that he could hit them again.

The children had a second beating and were then thrown in the water again. The evil young creature then left them and ran away. Luck was on the side of the victims, and a passer-by called George Crosby heard their cries and ran to help. The boy, called Patrick, was close to the side of the bank and he pulled him to safety. The girl had her feet stuck in the mud and he could see that she was frantically just managing to keep her head above the water. Crosby rescued both and then, as he knew them, he took them to the hut where their father was. Both were not so far from death – the girl had convulsions afterwards and at the time was near death with hypothermia. It is virtually certain that she would have died if a Constable Cowan had not been called and done some desperate first aid.

Cowan gave both a little brandy, sent for a surgeon, and then had the girl's body rubbed with salt. When Mr Lister, the doctor, arrived he saw the dangerously weak condition of the girl and later testified that without Cowan's quick-thinking she would have died. The child was fighting for her life for two days after this.

Mason was in court before justices Aldham and the bench a few days later and the case for the defence was that Mason was drunk and acted wildly and out of all character: he had, it was argued, drunk a pint of beer and eaten some mutton, but then met some other boys and shared a lot more beer with them followed by some gin. But the doctor, Lister, had been able to see him just after helping the victims because the police had brought him in and held him at the scene. He was sure that the boy was perfectly sober at that time. The police said that they had formed the same opinion. At that police Court hearing, the young criminal had stood impassive, saying nothing unless asked and then giving one-word replies.

Mason was committed for trial at the Leeds Assizes and there was an application for bail that was refused.

Events in recent times show that this kind of offence is always with us. In April 2009 there was a brutal attack by children on younger children in Yorkshire, and of course, the Jamie Bulger case of 1993 brought complicated issues of children and violence into public debate. In the mid-Victorian years there was a great deal of fear in the streets because of gangs of children, and this was to be a common feature of life, perhaps peaking in the 1890s with the arrival of the word 'hooligan' and a gang culture in London and other major cities. But there was also, as this case shows, the problem of children on the loose, doing mischief and damage to property, in many areas of the land. Mason's parents knew nothing of his activities as he was left to roam, join gangs and generally do as he pleased.

At Leeds, Justices Shee and Keating presided, and they had 103 people to attend to. Among the mass of adults waiting trial was young Mason. He was among five rapists, eleven killers, an arsonist, fourteen violent robbers and several other forgers and burglars. His case was listed in the causes- lists of charges – as 'attempt to drown.' At that time, the criminal law judged that a child between the years of seven and ten could not be guilty of a felony. The basic difference of felony and misdemeanour remained in English law until 1967, and the only aspect of a felony that was to change happened just four years after Mason's trial, when the forfeiture of estates and possessions of a felon was abolished.

One report noted that the law judged a child to be incapable of crime – an inaccurate statement, and something that showed the journalists could not cope with the repercussions of such a heinous crime. Technically, he was older than ten (he was ten years and nine months old) but this was disregarded. The report in The Manchester Times responded to the case with 'One case in the calendar however, was of a very peculiar character.' That understatement hints at the inability to explain matters.

In the language of the law, what could still have happened was that the jury could find that Mason had committed a 'mischievous discretion' asserting that he knew what he was doing and that he knew it to be wrong. If they agreed on that, then a 'true bill' was formed against the child. This means that there was a case to answer in court. This happened, and the original charge was changed to grievous bodily harm. For an adult that would have had serious consequences and would have meant a long time in gaol doing hard labour. But for a ten-year-old child some other solution had to be found.

Mason returned to court a week later to hear the decision and this time, at Leeds Town Hall, he was given a sentence of fourteen days in prison, followed by five years in a reformatory. He was told directly: 'Had you been a man you would have been severely punished.'

There was one very odd feature of Mason's trial – that it happened in an adult court. In 1847 the Juvenile Offences Act ruled that young people under fourteen should be tried in a special court. Maybe Yorkshire had not caught up with legal changes in 1886, but a more likely explanation is that the authorities wished to instil a profound fear into the boy; after all, British criminal legislation has never quite applied to the real situations of gaols throughout history. Even in the 1980s there were some prisons in England in which young offenders mixed with old convicts on wings.

The short gaol term was to provide a shock: to instil fear into the lad. Two weeks in Armley with hardened offenders would have been intended to shock and horrify him regarding the consequences of breaking the law. As to the reformatory, that was another matter entirely. By the time Mason had done the unspeakably cruel acts of torment to the little children, there had been a reformative movement established across the country. This meant that there was a separate system of juvenile justice. Mason would have been absorbed into something lying between a young offenders' institution and a disciplined factory (as Borstal did not arrive until the early twentieth century).

The normal practice in dealing with juvenile crime was whipping and beating. One influential opposite line of thought was expressed by Mary Carpenter when she said it was necessary to make young offenders feel 'the brotherhood of man.' In the years c.1840-1870 there was what one historian has called 'a preoccupation with the children of the dangerous classes.' In the case of young Frederick Mason, he had been left free to roam, to indulge in exerting his power over those weaker than himself, and then he had fallen in with a gang who were drinking and roaming the streets and fields. The parallels with modern 'ASBO' culture are clear: the criminological answer lies in parental and community order and cohesion. Mason was left free to go either good or bad, and the parents were nowhere on the scene through the criminal process, except at the back, well out of sight, leaving everything to the officials.

We have no knowledge of Mason's future course of life, but his years in a reformatory would have meant long hours of hard work, vigilance over him at all times, and physical punishment if required. The same principles that were applying solitary confinement and forced time for 'inner reflection' were placed alongside work in order to change attitudes and hopefully to rehabilitate into society.

Reformatory schools were established in 1854, specifically for offenders under the age of sixteen; they were often beaten and punishments were severe, but we have to recall that around forty years before the Mason case, children of his age who committed a crime as serious as his would sometimes be hanged. In 1819 a girl called Hannah Bocking, aged sixteen, had been hanged at Derby and as late as 1831 a teenager had been hanged in Coventry for murdering her uncle. Extreme serious crime by teenagers was to remain a problem with regard to capital punishment even into the 1930s: in 1931 a sixteen-year-old was sentenced to death for murder, though he was later reprieved.

Matters of Style
Running the risk of generalising too vehemently, I would suggest that there are three varieties of 'true crime' style:
The heavy, informative
The quasi-fictional
The classic commentary
The heavy, informative is the approach that constantly informs and explains, reaching out with references to other subjects. This tends to

interweave legal concepts, actions in the crime itself and explanations of investigative or courtroom procedure. It tends to need such supports as digression, footnotes or brackets. But the core of this is to provide a full account of the subject. It also tends to assume knowledge in the reader also.

The quasi-fictional tends to foreground the drama, the human story and the shock factor. The style is rather filmic, episodic, placing the dynamic elements over the secondary aspects such as explanations of concepts or institutions. The appeal is similar to crime fiction.

The classic commentary is often a style with a reliance on the three-part structure of crime- arrest-closure, with most writing clustering around these, and less detail in the secondary matter. This lends itself to a re-examination of a famous/infamous crime of course. In fact, looking again at a mystery from the annals of real crime is usually a winner, and today we have such science as DNA and forensic entomology to make new notions about classic crimes more easily attainable.

A Note on Journalism and Documentary

Naturally, because true crime is within the overall category we tend to call creative non-fiction today, it may be written so that it tells a crime story but in the guise of some other genre. A moment's reflection on some classic autobiography soon explains this: take Laurie Lee's autobiographical work, *Cider with Rosie*. This contains a chapter on a hangman and a crime. In the texture and substance of that amazingly sensual and imaginative work there is a crime story. Or take Ronald Blythe's *Akenfield*, a book dealing with the various inhabitants of that Suffolk village. Blythe has fascinating sections on the village policeman and the magistrate.

This is an element of documentary - something we use glibly in conversation but we forget that this word refers to both a genre and a style of writing. My own experience has taught me that a crime-related story will be there in any conversation, and sometimes, if we aim simply to write a documentary, meaning something documents a subject in a life or a community, there will be intriguing surprises. We only have to pause and consider how many people now retired were professionals in the various roles within the criminal justice system, to see the potential here. An article with a journalistic slant will of course put forward something that will inform, surprise, remind or analyse. In documentary there may be the same elements but there will also be a factor which includes an objective presentation of facts – material that leave an impact with the reader, something lacking a full commentary from you, the writer.

One of the simplest but most brilliant ideas in this category came from Connie Fletcher, who wrote a book called *What Cops Know* (see bibliography). Her sub-title was: 'cops talk about what they do, how they do it and what it does to them.' What Fletcher wrote in her preface to that book says something fundamental about crime writing: ' I became aware of the fact that police are privy to special knowledge, most of which they share only with other police… when my sister Julie became a police officer ten years ago, suddenly my family were given a glimpse of a world that was all around us and yet invisible to us.'

That notion of private knowledge, together with the thought of the paradox of visible/invisible is a comment that explains the success of true crime. If the crime writer helps the reader to look into those sealed worlds, then the success will be built in, stemming from deep human curiosity.

Tutorial
The freelance writing of true crime, then, is an activity with a number of options in terms of where potential publication may lie. But

everything depends, ultimately, on why you want to write in the genre. At the centre of the craft there is the requirement of a body of knowledge, an acquaintance with matters such as courts of appeal, DNA sampling and the work of detectives. But true crime may take a moral perspective as well as a criminological one, and in some senses, everything written will be heavily political because crime and law and mixed with power relations as well as a basis in the fabric of social control and the maintenance of order in the state and community.

If you want to write in order to remind readers of the sheer unbelievably horrific nature of some extreme crimes, then the reasons are simple and the writing techniques rather one-dimensional; if you want to write in order to change related matters, then writing embedded in a sociological form may be for you. For instance two books on serial killers were published in 2007: Christopher Berry-Dee's *Face to Face with Serial Killers* and David Wilson's *Serial Killers*. The first deals with the author's meetings with 'the world's most evil men' and attempts to look at the subject from all sides, in a documentary and factual way; the latter is an analysis and has the sub-heading, 'hunting Britons and their victims 1960-2006' Wilson was formerly a prison governor. His book combines standard criminology with a strong and often slick style. Berry-Dee is open to everything that falls before him, a creative writer with research behind him.

This contrast illustrates the diversity in the genre, and it also shows that often there are obvious elements in the subject which have been ignored and need attention – such as the stories of the victims that Wilson tells. As was stressed in my preface, the best true crime titles in the bookshop may often be found in other parts of the store – usually in biography or in non-fiction in marginal subjects. One last example will show the sheer diversity and scope of writing with a documentary aim: Amanda Wait's book, *Marked Men* (see bibliography). This deals with prisoners' tattoos and the stories behind them. This contains such statements as: 'It says something about my personality –when I make my mind up to do summat I do it. I'm not scared to risk things, to get hurt. Cause if you don't try, nowt ventured, nowt gained, do you know what I mean?'

****

8

RESEARCHING FOR A BOOK

One-Minute Summary

Once the decisions have been made about genre and specific sub-genre, then there are several ways of working. But today, the common practice is to attract a publisher or editor with the idea, so a letter of enquiry is the first step. This should have a little about yourself, a summary of the kind of book you have in mind and some thoughts on any competition already in print. After that a synopsis is needed.

The practicalities need to be considered too. A book in this genre needs research and time to absorb the basic material so that decisions about content may be made, and also, time to settle on the narrative voice you wish to use. The above reflections on how crime stories may be structured come back into view at this point. To put it simply, along the whole spectrum of possibilities, the options will range from sensational at one extreme and densely factual at the other.

A workable method is to write a summary for each chapter in advance. When you approach the publisher, you will then be able to supply a breakdown of material as it will be organised in each chapter. This approach will also give the publisher an insight into the scope and structure of the book at a glance. In the Edwardian period it used to be a tradition in textbooks to provide a summary of events at the opening of each chapter. In fact in his classic work of comedy, *Three Men in a*

Boat, Jerome K Jerome does exactly that. It might look something like this in a true crime book as a plan for one chapter:

Story	*legal material*	*social context*	*theoretical*
Serial killer	trial procedure	local community	crime mapping

Also in this section we look at some of the distinctions between crime history and true crime – more closely, and with examples.

The Synopsis

Rather than theorise, let's start with an example. I've invented this synopsis for a projected book on the prison in San Francisco bay, Alcatraz. Obviously, there have been several previous books on the prison. But the writing is about (a) knowing what is still in print and (b) being aware of previous treatments of the subject. On top of that, if the writer is absolutely sure what the new approach will be then explaining that to a publisher will not be difficult.

Here is the synopsis, based on a literature search in which I took time to see what was around in the marketplace, naturally, but also to express the difference I could offer, even if that difference is quite small. Anything on such a huge subject that offers a freshness in the narrative has some kind of chance of acceptance.

See overleaf.

Synopsis for a proposed book on Alcatraz

PUBLIC ENEMIES

America's hardest killers on the island fortress

Myself

I am a freelance writer and historian, working mostly in crime history and military history. I have written fifteen true crime books, most recently *Hanged at York* and *Square Mile Bobbies,* both for The History Press, *Britain's Notorious Hangmen* (Pen and Sword) and *Spies in the Empire* (Anthem Press). I'm currently completing a book on DNA and cold case files.

1. Rationale

We think of Alcatraz in Britain now and (a) older people or film buffs will think of the James Cagney era of black and white mobster films but (b) gangland literature and film noir movies have made the Capone era attractive to true crime readers more than ever before. Both prison life in the 30s-60s and the nature of gangs have a high media profile at the moment. Surprisingly, the first Alcatraz Governor had a very enlightened and humane view of his regime. But the hard men inside were still dealt with harshly and uncompromisingly where necessary.

The story of how Alcatraz was created is almost a book in itself – a massive logistic operation taking the hardest villains from across the whole of the States to San Francisco by train and then the last mile and a half by boat to the island.

There are plenty of general books on Alcatraz, predominantly published in the USA. My aim is to write the stories of 18 of these, including the 8 escapees. Obviously, the most famous and infamous figures on the list are Al Capone, Machine Gun Kelly and the Birdman, Robert Stroud.

The book will tell the story of how the prison was first created and the logistics of transporting the criminals from various state penitentiaries to San Francisco, and this will include an account of the Governor who did this, Warden James Johnston. The idea is to give a criminal biography of each villain and add details of the gangs they operated in where necessary.

It is also essential to include something on the island and prison itself, so the intention is to do this by summarizing each area and then specific cells where dramatic events happened.

2. Differentiation / Current Titles

I feel confident that there is a need for a strong narrative work on the Alctatraz hard men – particularly in Britain.

There are hundreds of books on Alcatraz, but the dozen most recent and forthcoming are concerned with the social history only, many of them about Alcatraz before it was the prison well known to modern readers. There have also been autobiographies by former prisoners, but these have been published in the USA. Works dealing with the stories of the prisoners are not so common and are mostly out of print, such as *Alcatraz, The Story Behind the Scenery* by James Delgado (1985) and *Riddle of the Rock – Escapes from Alcatraz* by Don Denevi (1991). The current top six titles are either graphic tales or picture books.

This book will have these features that are not presented in my format:

> ➤ Biographies and gangs summarised
> ➤ The story of the Governor and penal policy

> ➤ Accounts for British readers, explaining the American system and social history behind the crimes.
> ➤ Stories of lesser-known criminals
> ➤ Information on the firearms used

3 Chapter Breakdown

1. The Rock: a short history
2. The Man who Made Alcatraz
3. Al Capone
4. 'Machine Gun' Kelly
5. Roy Gardner
6. John Paul Chase
7. 'Doc' Barker
8. Henry Young
9. 'Creepy' Karpis
10. The Birdman
11. Clarence Carnes
12. Darwin Coon
13. Morton Sobell
14. 'Bumpy' Johnson
15. Mickey Cohen
16. Frankie Carbo
17. Irving Wexler
18. 'Whitey' Bulger
19. The Men Who Got Away
20. Screws Murdered

Bibliography and acknowledgements

Illustrations

Some, particularly portrait pictures, will be from archival material, but I have around 40 pictures taken at Alcatraz this year. I have cells, exterior shots, close-ups etc. I also have some other cultural iconic images such as the Al Capone Club in San Francisco and the bay area.

Schedule - to be in line with your requirements.

The synopsis is where the real effort should go before submitting an idea. Behind that there is the solid factual basis gained from finding materials in sources. In the resources section I have added a summary of archival records and legal sources. Basically, the chapter breakdown and synopsis provide a fairly accurate notion of the commercial potential of the book and they also indicate the kind of pre-thinking you have done. There are varying opinions in the writing community about what editors tend to read first, the synopsis or the sample writing. Editors and publishers will usually ask for a piece of sample writing, maybe a chapter. That should build rationally and clearly on the material in the synopsis.

Another useful tool to help in writing a synopsis is a blurb. Writing a 300-word blurb is a very useful test of your clear thinking. Look at some book cover blurbs of true crime books and it will be obvious what kinds of skills have gone into that writing: a blurb has to mix the essence of the synopsis with a direct message to the potential reader (and buyer) about the kind of read he or she is buying into if they take that book to the cashier.

Crime History and True Crime

There has already been a discussion of these varieties in my preface. But in the context of preparing a book, with the market place in mind, this is an ideal time to introduce the AQ. This is the author's questionnaire. Many publishers supply you with this, so that you do some marketing thinking. It asks for key features, intended readers and brief but succinct descriptions of style and content.

If we were to think of the differences in these two genres with an AQ in mind, we might have these kinds of contrasts:

CRIME HISTORY

➢ Plenty of awareness of the broader historical context

➢ Use of digression and explanation into the text

➢ More use of theoretical thinking

➢ General textual back-up: footnotes or end-notes

➢ Multiple inserts into the spine of the story

TRUE CRIME

➢ Tight focus on the human situation

➢ A slick, sharp narrative

➢ Very little in terms of sources

➢ A light touch in explanation- summaries of events

➢ A low level of assumed knowledge in the reader

In the most successful books in these genres of recent years (2008-9) it has become clear that there is a large and growing readership for books that mix both genres.

Tutorial

In this chapter we have turned to look at some practical applications of the planning and thinking behind the thoughts and suggestions of the first chapters. It should now be clear that the foundation for all this, in terms of planning and writing a true crime book, is a progression from initial idea to a statement of the rationale and scope of the projected book. A final word is needed on questions for yourself.

In writing workshops I have always found it useful to suggest and practise asking questions about the book being planned, starting with this little task:

In no more than one sentence, express the nature of the book, using these first words:

This book is about..and
....

To fill in those blanks means that there has been some lucid thinking. For example, you might have, 'This book is about a gang culture and one fatal decision by a man with power.' Or in a crime history work there could be: 'This is a book about a repressive government and one man's attempt to start a trade union.'

9

BIOGRAPHICAL PERSPECTIVES

One-Minute Summary
We now shift focus to what options are there in true crime for making the main focus biography. There are several categories in this corner of the market:

The biography of a well-known figure (villain, lawyer, policeman etc.)
An account of a group, gang (Mafia story etc.)
The story of a person who is unknown but whose life has been significant

Ghost Writing
The first three involve your own research and the last one depends on contact with a publisher. Publishers are always looking for ghost-writers for celebrities, but the business is now becoming more competitive. If this might be your kind of thing, then write or e-mail a publisher who tends to produce biographical crime works.

For the other three, everything demanded of the writer here is the same across the options: the aim is to produce a life story. But on top of that there are different possibilities.

Biography is always crucially important in the genre, and the reason is not hard to find: the key word is *motivation*. The question why is at the core of the narrative.

Biographical Examples

Here are three short extracts to illustrate the point.

(a) *Leeds' Female Serial Killer?*

It was just before Easter when Louie left the Waterhouse home, and Lily had been seen going into her house one Wednesday night around that time; but in those terraces neighbours saw and heard a great deal; there was very little privacy and people were sensitive to any unusual sounds. Domestic arguments would be heard by several neighbours, for instance. On this occasion, a neighbour heard noises in the lodger's room and then saw Louie as she left the house, carrying her baby. She told the neighbour that Lily was upset, but that she (Louie) was going home. She explained the odd noises by lying that she and Lily had been moving a bed.

At last Arty Calvert had his wife back, and also what he thought was his baby, little Dorothy. There was a happy time of course, and they were up late. But the next morning Arty saw that there was some luggage in the house that had not been there the night before. Unbelievably, Louie Calvert had returned to Amberley Road in the early hours and had collected this large suitcase; at this stage in her career, Louie was clumsy. She was seen by several people, despite the early time of day, and these sightings would be valuable statements later on in the tale. Even more surprising as we re-read the case today, she left a note. If she had not done that, then the chances are that the dual life she had constructed may well have kept her anonymous when the police started looking for the little woman who had lodged in Amberley Road.

They did indeed start looking for her, very soon after her dawn appearance at the lodgings, and this was because Lily Waterhouse had, of course, started a paper trail for the police when she summonsed her tenant. When Lily did not appear for that, the police came to check on her. *What they found in her home was the woman's corpse, lying on the floor in a bedroom; there was plenty of her blood in evidence around the body, even to the extent that some blood had splashed on the wall. She had been battered on the head as there was dried blood clotted on her scalp.*

The hallmark was there at the scene, though it was not perceived at the time: Lily Waterhouse was fully dressed – apart from her boots. There had been a violent struggle and the old lady had fought with some tenacity, as she was badly bruised, and it had taken several heavy blows to finish her. It is somewhat difficult to accept, bearing in mind the physical stature of Louie, that Lily Waterhouse had also been strangled. The killer, the police noticed, had cut up cloth to use to tie hands and feet...

(b) The First City Police Boss

Harvey was a complex man, with a chequered history at the time. He was born in 1786 in Witham, Essex. His father was a merchant banker and his mother was a daughter of Major John Whittle of Feering House, Kelvedon. Harvey stepped into Feering House in 1807 and worked as a country solicitor after his marriage to Mary Johnston of Bishopsgate Street. He was often involved in litigation, including a case of slander with another lawyer, a man called Andrew; after he was admitted to the Middle Temple he then applied for the Bar and he was rebuffed. Twice, over a period of twelve years, Harvey was rejected by the benchers and even a Select Committee of the House of Commons could not change that. The benchers thought him to be a man of questionable integrity; but as it happens, reports of the two trials he had been involved in were later deemed inaccurate, so Harvey was wronged and his career consequently suffered. The Select Committee of the Inns of Court reported on his case in 1834 and cleared his name.

Unlike Richard Mayne, his counterpart in the Metropolitan Police, then, Harvey was a man with a background in controversy and enmity; Mayne had been a provincial lawyer, working on the Northern Circuit when called for interview by Peel. Harvey had even been prosecuted for libel – successfully- in 1823, stating that George III was insane. Harvey served a prison term in the King's Bench.

But well before the establishment of the City Police, Harvey was busy in other things; he worked as a member of the common council of the City for ten years, and he was elected MP for Colchester in 1818, then in 1835 he was elected for Southwark. He became a known radical and was still often in busy, sensational cases and in business until his appointment as Commissioner. He was the man who took possession of the Sunday Times and sold it for a profit; he controlled the paper, The True Sun for seven years. As he was constantly in financial difficulties, the prospect of the salary of Police Commissioner must have seemed to him a very attractive prospect. He had already taken on another role, as registrar of metropolitan carriages, in 1839.

Both extracts show that there is an attempt to provide personality commentaries – the first on a twisted killer with obsessions and no scruples, ands the second on a man who attained great power but who had an eventful life before that success. Notice how the first has to concentrate on these character features and on the actual killing. The second has the pace to take in extra information. It is writing that is trying to deepen a study of a person who was important in history for several reasons but who was basically controversial. The first is more orthodox true crime.

Local and National

To return to the account of case books of crimes, this is a good point to stress the appeal and importance of a close focus on a group or community. Even in a true crime book that deals with a national subject, there will always be a local or regional hook in the story. The main difficulty arises when the research for a story depends on whether or not you can actually easily visit scenes of crime and talk to people with memories of the crime. This contrast from my own case book will illustrate the point.

(a) The Keith Lyon Case

This murder, unsolved, happened in Brighton. I sit in my study in Yorkshire. The logistical problems are evident for anyone to see. I needed to write a chapter for a book, with the focus on DNA work with regard to the case. Not only did I need pictures from the time, but really I needed to talk to or read about the forensic scientists involved, the detectives in the cold case team, and hopefully relatives or friends. None of this was available in any depth. I had to use the internet and follow up secondary sources, finding out information by indirect means. All I had was the archives I could find in general terms, such as newspaper reports.

I had just enough to write the chapter – if I added surmise and speculation, part of the stock in trade of the crime writer.

(b) On My Doorstep

Just a short drive from me was the place where a homicide had happened more recently. I could talk to people, read the local papers on microfiche and actually stand at the spot where the crime happened. An extract from what I wrote will illustrate a few important matters:

Ramshaw found her body when he returned from the night-shift at six in the morning, after leaving his home at nine-thirty the previous evening to be on time for the ten'oclock shift. He found her body in the kitchen, the gas light being still on. Police initially reported that there had been no signs of a struggle and that Ramshaw thought no money had been stolen. But it later emerged that a blood-stained breadknife was found that that is was likely that Emily tried to defend herself.

From the very beginning, these factors were to make this a puzzling case, as the death was the result of extreme violence and the motive was not clear. Unusually, the back door of the house was unlocked, and there were pots on the table, and if she had been entertaining a guest, then she had not changed into any new clothes, as she still wore her working-clothes.

Ravendale Street at that time was surrounded by other dwellings, bordered by an optician and a services canteen. The kitchen faced onto the back yard and the ten-foot fence, the latter still existing today, though Ramshaw's house is now part of a shop, and bricked-in windows that were part of number four may still be seen. An important detail is that the sitting room was visible from the main thoroughfare of Ravendale Street.

A post-mortem was carried out by Dr J M Webster of the Home Office and this was not available at the inquest on 24 September, so at that stage witnesses were called, and the high drama unfolded across the town as people read that top Scotland Yard officers were in town. Chief Inspector Davis and Sergeant Wolf were present, alongside Scunthorpe man, Superintendent Knowler. The coroner then gave more details, describing the state of Emily Charlesworth when found, with her head severely battered. Her face was so badly damaged then Ramshaw only *recognised her by means of her green jumper and the shape of her figure. The niece, Edna Warner, was also present.*

Harry Ramshaw talked about his last words to Emily as he left for work; she had said it was time for him to catch his bus and then she said, 'Do be careful Harry.' This was a reference to the risks involved in his work.

Clearly, attention turned to whether or not there might have been a visitor to Emily that evening. Her niece and Harry both said that this was unlikely. Edna Warner made a point of saying how happy and cheerful her aunt had been about a month earlier when she had last seen her. Even so early in the investigation, there were difficulties, and all the police could say was that they were following a line of enquiry. The pathologist's report was desperately needed.

Meanwhile, a fingerprint expert, C I Birch and a crime scene photographer, D I Law, also came north from the Yard. The whole enquiry was escalating. The local reports were fragmented at this early stage, and papers were eager to snap up any little detail. Some said that a neighbour had heard a scream; another that a vital clue had been found but was not sure what that was. The coroner, Mr Dyson, was told by Knowler that it would be some weeks before the police were in a position to pass on any definitely important information.

The important point here is the reference to Ravendale Street. Of course, it would be hard work to find that local knowledge without being there. Wherever possible I try to go to the scene of crime and I look and feel my way into the nature of the place: this is not to suggest any psychic 'vibes' but I have come to believe that the best true crime writing has a quality of empathy, in which the writer tries to recreate the victim's state of mind from available facts.

111

Your resources from the locality – from people, places and written, paper sources are:

Conditions at the time – the topography/climate/ economics etc.
The local context (newspapers are invaluable)
Available oral history/anecdotes
Your own intuition and imagination
Biography is at the heart of this.

Revisiting the Past

Again, an example will help here. Even the most recent crime stories reach into the past, and they are embedded in a location. It might be said that there is an emotional epicentre to the criminal act; why else do certain places resonate – such as 10, Rillington Place or Cromwell Road? There will always be a tainted perspective on writing about the crimes that took place there. True crime is in many ways another version of social history, but it opens up certain perspectives which are just not available or possible in other modes of writing. The following extract is from an unsolved case, and it demonstrates something of this special kind of 'revisiting.' There is empathy and knowledge – both applied to a time and a place.

This is an extract from my book, Cold Case Investigators, about DNA in cold case file work. It relates to an unsolved murder from over sixty years ago. The main topic here is the dilemma of the man who recalls the case and how he has lived all his life with the dark shadow of being suspected of the crime.

The DNA revolution will at least free people from blame, even if the killer is found and has died. The evidence will achieve several things, but mainly it will exonerate suspects. One of these, arguably the main suspect at the time, is Hubert Hoyles, now seventy-five years old.

He was the last person to see Muriel alive, and he was interviewed in November, 2008. Hubert was formerly a factory worker but on that fateful day in 1946 he was the person who had bought eggs from Margaret Drinkwater, walking past the girl as she walked home. He said, ' I'd usually see Muriel as she made her way from school and we'd exchange a hello... I saw her that day. She was just minutes from her house when we crossed on the path near the woods where she was killed.' Hubert has been swabbed and exonerated, after all those years – years in which he has had to suffer the feelings that people were talking about him behind his back.

Hubert was just thirteen at the time, and he recalls Muriel as being lovely, and always happy; he told reporters that ' I've lived with the knowledge that some people in this community suspected me.. I knew in the eyes of some people I was the murderer. It blighted my life.' It was noted in the interview with him that over the years he has never spoken of the murder, except to police and a little to his wife; it seems highly likely that Hubert actually passed the probable killer, because he recalls that a few weeks before her death he passed a man in the exact spot where the murder was to be done. He said, ' I'd been up to the farm one afternoon when, at exactly the spot along the route... a smartly dressed man in his thirties suddenly emerged without noise from the bushes.' If that was indeed the killer, then if he were alive today, assuming he was thirty then, he would be ninety-nine years old today. Hubert recalled that 'There was a menace about him. A wickedness.'

In order to write this, I had to revisit the past with Hubert's words, together with the relation of the usual objective facts. The result was an approach that fused the man's actual words with a hint about his inner

113

feelings and a suggestion that he was not the only one: that a cold case creates unease in several people, not only the unknown killer.

Interviews and Profiles

One version of popular true crime writing that never goes away is the short account of a person involved in a case – in a journalistic or impressionistic way. The clearest example from my own files is when I interviewed someone who was very much involved in the Moors Murders. My meeting with her was quite by chance, but since then she has spoken on TV about her experiences and also talked about other interests and experiences in her life.

The article I wrote based on that interview only touched the surface of what could have been said. After all, here was a person who had sat in an office with a typewriter as forensic samples such as bits of hair or tissue were brought in and placed on the desk. She was not a police officer at that time but did join the force shortly afterwards.

That might be an exceptional example, but the suggestion here is to make efforts to find out the people in your local area who have interesting past experiences of anything within criminal justice, police work or even a victim's experience. These may be very sad and even tragic of course, like the family in my area who still leave a light on every night, thirty years after the disappearance of their young daughter.

Some true crime writers – the ones who specialise in blood and suffering – would relish an interview with a criminal or a victim of course. But there is far more to crime writing than that. Even the everyday workers within the system have all kinds of tales to tell. Back in 1948 a man who had been a justice's clerk for thirty years wrote a book in which he related the cases he knew about. Every story he had was potentially a feature article for a crime writer. That book was self-published and is almost impossible to find now. He had tales of gangs, con-men, murders, car crime, fraud and every kind of violence one could imagine. He also had comic stories. That should not be forgotten. After all, one of the most common true crime experiences is crime gone wrong: a large proportion of robberies never happen because of incompetence, and prison stories are packed with dark humour.

But there is a market for profiles and interviews: the kind of short biography that may be written and integrated with a crime story. Of course, there is a moral perspective on this. I once met someone who knows one of the Yorkshire Ripper's victims – a woman who survived an attack. Both my friend and the person herself work hard to preserve anonymity. There have even been cases where writers have tried to gain access to serial killers in gaol by assuming a false identity and contacting the killer asking for a visiting order to be issued.

There is a seedy side to true crime writing, and some of this kind of thing borders on the criminal itself: desperation and the amoral, stop-at-nothing approach rarely pay off.

Tutorial

Biography is very important in a true crime story. To bring out a full account of the people involved in the case may be a challenge, but it is worth the effort. Even cases from the distant past suggest such matters as mental illness and debates and issues about motive and personality that were not understood at the time. A case in Lincolnshire in late Victorian years involved the killing of a police constable. The man who did the deed had a serious mental illness, and it was only when a medical specialist picked up the story that anything happened in law: the result was that the killer went to an asylum rather than to the noose.

10

PROFESSIONAL KNOWLEDGE

One-Minute Summary

In support of true crime writing there is a huge body of knowledge. The genre is done on a foundation of knowledge stemming from criminal law, social history, social science, the history of medicine, forensics and linguistics. Any single case may demand research in any or all of these disciplines. My own writing has entailed regular consulting of reference works and sometimes necessitated contacting specialists to be sure that I have the facts right. As was noted in the chapter on research, there is a vocabulary as well as this body of knowledge, and this is the cement for the brickwork of the writing.

The best advice I have is to start with a conception of the legal process in criminal law and a sense of what police work entails.

I have acquired this knowledge in the course of writing. I have done no degree in law or criminology. The main demands on me when writing this genre are of empathy, deduction and insight into human motivation, but all this is on top of the knowledge base. The main categories you will need to have at your fingertips are these, and this is based on Dr Johnson's famous maxim that there are two types of knowledge: that which we know and that which we can find out:

The language of law

Criminological concepts

Key legislation in social and political history

Medical terms
Forensic concepts
Personality as interpreted and defined by psychology

The best advice is to reiterate the need for reference works, and I have listed these in my bibliography and resources section at the end of this book. But of course we also have the internet, and this is a wonderful resource, though it has to be used with care and facts need to be double-checked. For that reason it is worth investing in reference works, even though they may be expensive.

Issues and Debates
In 2008 I gave a talk on true crime at a bookshop, and I openly admitted that I was a passionate amateur, but not the kind who relishes the blood and gore. I approach the subject from the standpoint of an historian and I see true crime as a branch of that, with a healthy dose of social science. But increasingly now the books are being written by writers with a background in the biological sciences. The contrast between the varying sorts of writers is part of the arena in which the subject is debated. Some of the most exciting and dramatic true crime works have been written by such people as novelists, journalists and complete enthusiasts with no qualifications from universities. These tend to be the controversial topics, and you need to make up your own mind on each of these:

The morality in the genre
If we accept that crime has a moral and a political dimension, then it might be argued that creative writers may do more harm than good when entering the fray, so to speak. The argument goes that an amateur will perhaps have the knowledge but has no professional ethics. The

clearest way to see this is to contrast two writers, one who may be a forensic scientist and the other a creative writer or journalist. Look at the different approaches they might use to a similar subject. All the large-scale crime stories have been written about by both types of writer, so look at books on these topics for instance: Dr Crippen, Jack the Ripper, serial killers, cannibalism, the Yorkshire Ripper, John Christie, The Wests and Ted Bundy. Any comparison made on any one of these will quickly show the differences.

But does this mean that one is less successful because it lacks assumed ethical codes?

A Matter of Politics and Bias

It might be said that creative writers and journalists who work in this genre may create undesirable consequences after their work is in print: such matters as moral panics, distortions of the facts, bias and twisted interpretation may occur. Maybe bias is unavoidable, even in works written by qualified professionals?

Distorted Information and Errors

Being amateurs, true crime writers are open to the charge of making errors and giving the wrong information. There is one simple remedy – ask a professional to look over any part of your book that deals with technical knowledge.

The Trade Vocabulary

As stated earlier in this chapter, there is what might be called a 'trade vocabulary' in the genre, and this is the mix of language and terminology coming from the academic and professional areas we have to tap into in order to write at all. Rather than theorise about this, I now offer a piece of crime writing and have written in bold the 'trade vocabulary:

In 1857 **Baron** Martin, a judge who had begun his career at **the bar** rather later than usual at the age of twenty-nine, found himself sitting at the **Surrey Assizes** with a very nasty and brutal killing of a police detective presented before him. Baron Martin was much respected as a lawyer who understood mercantile affairs and he was in demand at the Guildhall as well as in Liverpool and the Northern Circuit. He was remembered as the **judge who never had a** *remanet* – a term used for a second sitting at the **Queen's Bench.** In other words, he got on with things and had a practical, no-nonsense turn of mind.

The case before him was that of the murder of Detective Charles Thain, who had been shot on board the Caledonia, while sailing back to England from Hamburg. The man who shot and killed him was Christian Sattler, a desperate character who had been born in France but followed a military career in Germany before landing in England and starting a career of crime.

In the trial, Benjamin Eason, chief warder at the Wisbech gaol, remembered Sattler well. He said that the man had been on remand for a week and then convicted for a **petty theft**. But the warder's recalled conversation with Sattler was a significant one. He said that he advised Sattler, on release, to 'endeavour to obtain an honest livelihood' and he opined that the good Christian people of England would not allow him to starve if he could not find any work. Sattler replied, 'It's not a Christian country, I will not ask for relief; if I cannot get employment I will thieve, I will steal, and if anyone attempts to prevent me, I will shoot him like a dog.' The man was fond of that last phrase. He was to repeat it on board the *Caledonia* when he had shot Thain. Eason was asked to report on the **accused**s general attitudes and submission to the gaol discipline and he could bring to mind merely one small misdemeanour that cost his extra hard labour for an hour. But otherwise, he was not exactly recalled as a crazed sociopath.

At the Mansion House at the first hearing the charge was put explicitly and clearly: chief clerk Samuel Goodman repeated it later before Martin: ' For shooting on the high seas at 4.15 p.m. on the 22nd instant, detective sergeant Charles Thain in the right breast, with intent to murder the said officer.' There were plenty of witnesses, and it soon became clear what had happened. The story began with Sattler stealing a carpetbag with clothes and cash in it; he pawned the clothes in Cambridge and then made for London, and the man who had been robbed was a stockbroker in the city. Sattler found at the trial that all kinds of people came forward and soon the narrative of his escape from Cambridgeshire to London was closely documented.

A pawnbroker in Cambridge, for instance, Robert Cole, stated in court that Sattler had gone to his house to pawn a mackintosh and had pledged it for five shillings in the name of Pickard. Cole, after Sattler had returned with banknotes to buy a watch, was suspicious and checked the notes; then he heard about the robbery and told the police. Information was given to the City police and two detectives, Jarvis and Thain, were on the case. It became a fast-paced pursuit, as Sattler had gone from his lodgings in Gracechurch Street and the sleuths found out that he had been heading for Hamburg. They set off in pursuit.

Thain got his man in Germany, and the next records we have of this pursuit is from the first mariner witness, Stephen Robertson, at the trial. He said,

' On 20th November last I embarked on the Caledonia at Hamburg for London – I had been shipwrecked and was a Consul passenger... I did not see the prisoner personally until till he was down below... I was standing on the gangway a little after ten o'clock... the

120

deceased officer, Thain, came on board by himself – three other gentlemen behind him – the prisoner came on board after Thain accompanied by two gentlemen.'

He saw Sattler later, in his cabin, handcuffed. Thain had been given a small separate cabin and he was by all accounts looking after Sattler, as many seamen commented 'with kindness.'

The stories given by various witnesses built up a picture of Sattler as a moaning complainer, irritating those around him and yet being well cared for by the detective. Robertson heard Thain speak and respond to Sattler's request that his handcuffs be taken off, as they were giving him considerable pain. He heard Thain say, 'I have been warned of you, but I will take them off when we get to England, if you behave yourself.' Robertson heard the gunshots at around four in the morning of the Sunday (Thain and Sattler had boarded on the Friday night). This was the scene before him as he ran into the cabin: ' .. the prisoner was sitting on a chest, Thain was standing up, holding on to him with one hand, and with the other at his own breast. He said, "The prisoner has shot me" – I seized hold of the prisoner and dragged him out of the cabin.'

There was then a very nasty scene, after Sattler had explained why he had shot. He said simply that Thain had not been a man of his word. He had loaded his concealed pistol by the side of his bed and then shot at Thain as he came in. He said that Thain had not 'kept his word as a gentleman' and had said earlier that he would 'shoot like a dog' any man who broke his word. A gang of seamen on board, led by some American sailors, grabbed Sattler and some were for lynching him there and then. Some shouted that they wanted to 'stretch' him, meaning to pull hard on all his joints as a torture, and then hang him. A Mr Lilley described the situation: ' ... he was dragged on deck rather roughly; they did not handle him very softly... he was not in a very excited state at this time, he only cried out with the pain of his arms being pinioned behind him. He had the handcuffs on and a handkerchief was placed around the muscles on his arm.' The gunman was then tied hard to a large bolt on the fore hatch.

As for Thain, he had not yet expired when the *Caledonia* docked that Sunday. He was taken to Guy's Hospital and there he made a statement for the magistrate. He wrote that 'at about twenty minutes before four o'clock I got up and left the cabin and went to the water closet, having locked up the cabin and left him there. I returned in about a quarter of an hour and found him sitting on a folding carpet stool.' Thain asked if Sattler wanted any tea, and as the man answered in the negative, Thain turned with a folded coat, and then he was shot.

Other police officers gave testimony and it emerged that not only had Sattler hidden a gun on his person, but he also had a knife, and told one man that he thought about knifing Thain earlier but changed his mind.

Thain died on 4 December and the house surgeon, Alexander McDougal said he found three pistol balls on the officer. He showed the balls to the court and said that he was holding up a piece of the man's diaphragm with the ball in it. When asked about the likely position of the deceased when shot, he thought that Thain would have been stooping when shot. Detective Jarvis, who came to the dock and found his colleague lying there severely wounded, said that he asked Sattler to show him how he managed to fire the gun while wearing the handcuffs, and that Sattler demonstrated how he had done that. The killer told Jarvis that he had estimated the powder required: 'There might have been enough in the pistol for two, three or four charges..'

The defence counsel had obviously reasoned that Sattler's only chance of escaping the noose was to argue that **the custody was illegal**. The court report gives the man's account in this way:

'*Mr Lilley then proceeded to content that the prisoner was not in legal custody; that his apprehension was forced and unlawful; that being a foreigner he was not amenable to the English law; that no proof had been offered as to whether or not any treaty or convention with Hamburg was in existence and therefore.... The arrest was clearly wrongful.*'

Notice that the early part of the piece has a great deal of legal terminology. The point is that it would be ridiculous to explain all of these in the text – note that I did so on just one occasion. Footnotes would also be an irritation to the reader. Certain terminology may be assumed, but there is always a vagueness(what exactly would the 'gaol discipline' have been?).

Case Studies
Here are some short extracts with notes on the base knowledge being used, again with terms in bold:

Bow Street Ruuners
The Runners were fundamentally for hire and found their work extremely lucrative. The group of Runners took their share in the money distributed among any group of witnesses who had played a part in a conviction for a felony; they averaged £20 a year from this. In addition, they received items called **Tyburn tickets**. These were exemption tickets from more onerous work as a constable across the city; they were valuable and made around £20 when sold. One of the best-known Runners, Townsend, along with some colleagues, managed to operate as a **special security unit,** guarding royalty, opera-houses and clubs. After George III had been attacked as he stepped down from his coach in St James's Palace in 1786, a woman called Margaret

Nicholson came forward and made a lunge at the King's chest with a knife. The King played this down and showed some understandable sympathy for her, saying she was 'mad.' But after that, what we would now call special duties by detectives – guarding the sovereign – were undertaken by Townsend. He received a huge sum of £200 a year for these special duties, and Townsend became very popular with the king.

Yet the Runners did establish many of the common practices of later professional detectives in their methods of work. Their visits to 'flash houses' for instance, in which they cultivated their informers, were essential to their limited success. They learned, by trial and error, to create a range of good information sources and to have a few key contacts for immediate reference when anything of major importance happened, such as a kidnapping or a high-profile robbery.

The Ripper in Whitechapel

It can be seen, looking back at that time, that it was a period of accelerated change in terms of the new commuter class and of what the sociologist Durkheim has called 'anomie.' Traditional cohesion in working class communities steadily disintegrate, particularly in London and other major cities, and along with that came a more common occurrence of anomie – the sense of the identity and communal purpose being taken away, meanings and patterns of known justifications for actions being blurred. The years c. 1870-1890 were years in which the city was becoming a metaphor for this anomie and loss of community, a location for disenchantment, loneliness and **sociopathic feeling**. The gothic fiction such as Stevenson's explored the nature of transgression and disorder within the self, the closeness of barbarity to what Victorians were wont to dwell on as desirable 'civilisation.' After all, in 1857, the British Empire exercised its civilising qualities by firing cannon through the bodies of Indian mutineers and the British police in 1880 were handy with their truncheons for which a special new pocket had been introduced in 1887.

Here was the CID then, along with the detectives of Scotland Yard and of the City force, in most senses still having the same ideology of policing as their uniformed colleagues: military still but now with detective methods which in many ways paralleled the methods of military espionage as practiced first against political radicals and later against the enemy in the outposts of empire. Their knowledge at the time when the Ripper appeared was practical, but also locked into the crimes emanating from community, not from forces alienated from that community. Worse still, the Ripper killings were on prostitutes, seen then as a sad but necessary industry for those women fallen and still falling.

A Hanging

We know a lot about the last days of James Murphy in York before he was hanged, because the hangman, James Berry, kept a journal and published his memoirs. He even managed to joke about his impending death. Murphy, from Barnsley, was a collier from Lambert's Fold, Dodsworth and he had twenty-five convictions for poaching. Murphy, full of vengeance, set out one day to look for a police officer called Austwick, and he shot the man dead. He was cornered and arrested in Barnsley, but there was a local groundswell of feeling that he did not deserve to hang, as it was thought that the crime was done on the spur of the moment, and not premeditated. An appeal for a reprieve failed.

When Berry came to have his chat in the **condemned cell**, Murphy said he would not give the hangman any trouble: 'I am not afraid to die. A lot of people have been making a fuss about me. But I'm hanged if I can see what there is to make a fuss about.' Berry was impressed by the sick joke. Murphy had to walk past his own waiting grave on the way to the scaffold and all he said to Berry was that he wanted him to do it 'as painlessly as you can.'

Berry's note in his journal was, ' I hanged James Murphy in spite of threats and then I heard that I would never dare set foot in Barnsley, the town whence the victim hailed. People said that the Barnsley miners would murder me, but in spite of the threats I visited the town on many occasions.' Usually, Berry was happy to enjoy his notoriety and the fact that the media took an interest in him. In Leeds, the printer Charles Johnson produced a biography of Murphy in a **chapbook,** with the title, *The Life of James Murphy the Barnsley Murderer*, and it meant that the killer would be the first name linked to the town in that way. The picture of Murphy on the cover of the book shows a calm, ordinary man with arms folded, as if waiting for a conversation about the weather. Virtually every term in bold could potentially be explained, expanded and developed into further commentary and explanation. The important thing to note is the place in which explanations are given in the text. Also, the theoretical terms such as 'anomie' which of course, have definitely to be explained in the text as mentioned.

Tutorial

To sum up, the important points about the base knowledge of true crime writing falls into these topics:

Essential vocabulary and concepts (e.g. you must know what an indictment is and what is meant by an assize court or a crown court.

Theoretical Basis: the abstract concepts relating to psychology or biology – and even some examples of physiology in forensics – need to be easily accessible in works written for the layman, not the specialist.

General historical and biographical details: easy access to these dictionaries/encyclopaedias is also essential.

REFERENCE SECTION
1

The legal System and Crime

'There were growing concerns in eighteenth-century England over crime and disorder. For the traditional police historians these growing concerns reflected a growing reality... But is it extremely difficult to measure any increase in levels of crime even in a society which keeps statistics, and eighteen –century England kept none. There is some agreement among the historians of crime in eighteen-century England, based on the study of indictments and other court records, that larceny probably was increasing; the statistics which the government began to collect from 1805 also show an increase continuing until the middle of the nineteenth century.'

Clive Emsley   *The English Police: A Political and Social History* 1991

Larceny: theft. But larceny was more limited than theft, and needed a carrying away of property (asportation)

Capital crimes –for which the death sentence would be inflicted – were arson; burglary; beast-stealing; coining forgery; highway robbery; house-breaking; horse-stealing; murder; manslaughter; privately stealing; rape; robbery in a dwelling house; robbing the mails; robbing the post office; rioting; stealing in a dwelling house; shop-lifting; sheep-stealing; stealing on board ship, treason and unlawful shooting. By the eighteenth century, most types of theft were put together and called 'felony' – and became capital crime if the goods value taken was over 39 shillings. Felonies for less than that sum could still be capital crimes if they were double felonies (felonies aggravated by other misdemeanors)

Felony: until 1967- an offence more serious than a misdemeanor: it is helpful to think of indictable and summary offences. A summary conviction is done in a magistrate's court

Indictment – a case tried in a crown court. Most serious common law offences are indictable - murder, rape etc., and many are created by statute. If a statute does not specify how an offence is to be tried, then it is indictable. But some indictable offences may be tried, now, be tried by magistrates.

The basic operation of law involved:

The various courts, from local summary/magistrate sittings to quarter sessions and assizes.

No professional police force, so there were trading justices and thief-takers; then military action in extreme cases, and of course, citizens and witnesses.

Abuses such as the time waiting trial: the justices' duty of **oyez and terminer** and jail delivery

(Royal commissions to hear and determine cases of insurrection, murder, coining and other serious crimes within a county. Records were kept by Clerks of the Peace.)

The Courts

Magistrates' Court   'Maid of all work for the English legal system' (Peter Archer)

The roots go back to the establishment of unpaid justices of the peace appointed from 1277/1287 as 'keepers of the peace'. They were termed justicers by a statute of 1361. By 1565 there were 30-40 magistrates per county- dealing with minor matters in petty sessions and then attending jury trials at quarter sessions

Assize: until 1972, a periodical county session for civil and criminal justice. They were established in the early thirteenth century, initially to work towards uniting customs and common law. Two or more judges from London traveled a circuit, visiting the major towns three times a year. There were seven circuits, and the idea was to give locals the chance to have cases heard in regions rather than in London.

Quarter sessions: Courts founded in 1361, for quarterly meetings of justices. They started to meet at Easter, Midsummer, Michaelmas and Epiphany. (These were available to readers in the eighteenth century in papers and journals).

These sessions were criminal cases such as riot, poaching, murder and assault; in the Tudor period the justices were given greater powers. From 1531 they dealt with the administration of the Poor Law. They were advised in law by the Clerk of the Peace. In the eighteenth century these began to be held more often in some towns rather than others.

Two types: county quarter sessions: with a group of magistrates and borough quarter sessions (supervised by a barrister known as a recorder). From 1819, magistrates were allowed to sit separately and so two courts could function at the same time.

Assizes and quarter sessions overlapped, the assizes handling the more serious crimes.

Quarter sessions and assizes were replaced by the crown court in 1972

But in the eighteenth century, many minor matters were dealt with by **summary courts** (see Peter King: 'The Summary Courts and Social Relations in Eighteenth-Century England' in *Past and Present* number 183 May, 2004 pp. 125-169).

Later, police courts also took some of these functions.

Brief examples

Typical Old Bailey Session:

20 September 1752
Ended the sessions… when five persons received sentence of death for robbing and murdering Joseph Brown, a brewer's clerk; Thomas Butler for returning from transportation; John Wilks for street robbery and Matthew Lee for a highway robbery. Two others to be transported for 14 years, forty-seven for seven years; four to be whipped and three branded. There were 102 prisoners tried in all.

Newspaper reports:
A bill of indictment was found at Hick's Hall against four persons for feloniously demolishing the Star Tavern in the Strand, laid on the statute of 1 geo. I cap. 5 but the evidence not being ready, the trial was deferred to the next Sessions…..

Riotous attack on a turnpike
8 May, Selby, Yorks. The bellman made proclamation for the inhabitants to bring their hatchets and axes at 12 o'clock that night to

cut down the turnpike erected there by Act of Parliament. Accordingly the great gate with five rails was totally destroyed by some riotous persons, for discovery of whom the lords Justices have offered his Majesty's pardon to any person concerned, except the bellman, and a reward of £50 on conviction. And the commissioners of the turnpike have offered a further reward of £20.

Some Statistics   (from John Howard   *The State of the Prisons in England and Wales* 1777)

Crime stats:
Offences carrying the death penalty:
Horse-stealing   202
Burglary   93
Highway robbery   65
Other felonius crime 44
Petty treason and murder   20
Returning from transportation   6
Forgery   4

Total of felons condemned to death: 434
Of these:
Executed -   117
Reprieved for transportation - 308

Some documentary sources

At quarter sessions, paper was generated: records for lunatic asylums, bastardy, militia recruitment etc. But these are the typical categories of records to be found:

> Calendars of prisoners
> Recognizances
> Indictments
> Order books
> Judges' reports

(from prisons – various types of reports, from medical to punitive)

e.g. from 1629 to 1749 there were draft orders and memoranda books relating to quarter session rolls. From 1750, Order Books replaced Quarter Sessions Rolls.

Calendars of prisoners – lists of people held at various locations before trial. These provide name, age, crime, offence and date of arrest warrant.

Indictment rolls -names of offenders with offences

Recognizance Books -Mainly, bonds for appearance at the quarter sessions, to answer charges to prosecute, and with details of any supporting material brought to the trial.

2
Bibliography
Reference works
Butler, T R Fitzwalter, *The Criminal Appeal Reports* 1910-1955
          Sweet and Maxwell
Cyriax, Olivier, *The Penguin Encyclopaedia of Crime* Penguin, 1993
Donaldson, William, *Rogues, Villains and Eccentrics* Phoenix, 2002
Eddleston, John J. T*he Encyclopaedia of Executions* Blake, 2002

Evans, Stewart and Skinner, Keith, *The Ultimate Jack the Ripper Sourcebook* Robinson, 2002

Fido, Martin and Skinner, Keith, T*he Official Encyclopaedia of Scotland Yard* Virgin Publishing, 2000

Fielding, Steve, *The Hangman's Record: Volume One, 1868-1899* Chancery House Press, 1999

Friar, Stephen, T*he Sutton Companion to Local History* Sutton, 2001

Lane, Brian, *The Encyclopaedia of Forensic Science* Headline, 1992

O'Neal, Bill, *The Pimlico Encyclopaedia of Western Gunfighters* Pimlico, 1998

Woodley, Mick (Ed.) *Osborn's Concise Dictionary of Law* Thomson, 2005

Books on Crime writing

Turner, Barry (Ed.) *The Writer's Handbook Guide to Crime Writing* (Macmillan, 2003

Wynn, Douglas *The Crime Writer's Handbook* (Allison and Busby, 2003

Forensics

Ainsworth, Peter B *Offender Profiling and Crime Analysis* (Willan, 2001)

Moore, Pete T*he Forensics Handbook* (Eye Books, 2004)

White, P C *Crime Scene to Court: the essentials of Forensic Science* (Royal Society of Chemistry, 2004)

True Crime Works: a Select List

Bentley, David, *The Sheffield Hanged 1750-1864* Print and Design, 2002

Bentley, David, *The Sheffield Murders 1865-1965* Print and Design, 2003

Binding, Tim, *On Ilkley Moor* Picador, 2001

Bland, James, *True Crime Diary Vol. 2* Warner Books, 1999

Burnley, James *West Riding Sketches* Hodder and Stoughton, 1875

Campbell, Marie, *Curious Tales of Old West Yorkshire* Sigma, 1999

Campbell, Marie, *Strange World of the Brontes* Sigma, 2001

Cawley, A C (Ed.) *A Yorkshire Tragedy* Manchester University Press, 1986

Clarke, A A *Killers at Large* Arton Books, 1996

Cornwell, Patricia, *Portrait of a Serial Killer* Time Warner, 2002

Davies, Owen, *Murder, Magic, Madnes : The Victorian trials of Dove And the Wizard* Pearson, 2005

Dernley, Syd with Newman, David, *The Hangman's Tale* Pan, 1989

Ellis, John, *Diary of a Hangman* Crime Library, 1997

Emsley, Clive, *Crime and Society in England 1750-1900* Longman, 1996

Emsley, Clive, *The English Police A political and social history* Pearson 1991

Evans, Stewart P. *Executioner: The Chronicles of James Berry, Victorian* Hangman Sutton, 2004

Goodman, David, *Foul Deeds and Suspicious Deaths in Leeds* Wharncliffe, 2003

Gould, Russell, *Unsolved Murders* Virgin, 2002

Grey, D (Ed. S J Pimm) *The Facts Behind the Guardhouse Murder 1864* Whins Wood Publishing house, Keighley, 1996

Harrison, Paul *Yorkshire Murders* Countryside, 1992

Hovell, M, *The Chartist Movement* Manchester University Press, 1918

Hughes, Robert, *The Fatal Shore* Vintage, 2003

Humphreys, Travers, *Criminal Days* Hodder and Stoughton, 1946

Hunt, Tristram, *Building Jerusalem, The rise and fall of the Victorian City* Phoenix, 2004

Inglis, Brian, *Poverty and the Industrial Revolution* Panther, 1971

James, Mike, T*he Bedside Book of Murder* True Crime Library, 1998

Jones, Richard Glyn, *True Crime Through History* Constable, 2004

Low, Donald A *The Regency Underworld* Sutton, 2005

Pontefract, Ella, and Hartley, Marie, *Yorkshire Tour* Smith Settle, 2003

Porter, Roy, *English Society in the Eighteenth Century* Penguin, 1982

Porter, Roy, *Madness: A Brief History* Oxford, 2002

Rawlings, Philip, *Crime and Power: A History of Criminal Justice* Longman, 1999

Rowland, John *Unfit to Plead?* Pan, 1965

Stevenson, David *1914-1918 The History of the First World War* Penguin, 2004

Thomas, Donald, *The Victorian Underworld* John Murray, 1998

Thompson, E P *The Making of the English Working Class* Penguin, 1968

Thornton, David, *Leeds: Story of a City* Fort Publishing, 2002

Tobias, J J C*rime and Industrial Society in the Nineteenth Century* Penguin, 1972

Regional Crime History

As was mentioned with reference to the availability of lists of officers involved in newspaper reports, it has to be added that there is another way to find out fairly quickly if your police ancestor was involved in a crime story. This does not necessarily mean that he or she was part of the hunt for a mass murderer or that the name of the ancestor is going to be in major works of true crime. But it may mean that a quick check in the index of a series book from one of the specialist regional or local crime casebooks will have your officer featuring in a story.

There are five ongoing series from three different publishers currently being printed regularly, and these volumes are gradually covering most of the cities and towns of Britain and Ireland. The three main series are:

Foul Deeds and Suspicious Deaths	Wharncliffe/ Pen and Sword Publishers
County murders series	Countryside Books
Murder and Crime In... series	Tempus (The History Press)
County Murders	Tempus
Hanging chronicles	Tempus
Murders and Misdemeanours	Amberley (Formerly Sutton)

A typical description of what may be found in these books is in this summary of *Cumbria Murders* by Paul Heslop:

'*Cumbria Murders* brings together numerous murderous tales that shocked not only the county but also made headlines throughout the country...Paul Heslop was a policeman for over thirty years, mostly as a detective. His experience and understanding of the criminal justice system give authority to his unbiased   assessment and analysis of the cases...'

In the Wharncliffe *Foul Deeds and Suspicious Deaths* series there are all categories of crime covered, so there is more likelihood that ordinary police constables will have been caught up in the narrative of a particular offence, and more importantly perhaps, the constable concerned would often be someone who knew and lived in the community in which the crime occurred. As an example, a search of the index for my own volume on Halifax (2004) finds twelve officers of various ranks embroiled in the action, as were these two men in a murder case from 1909: ' Two sergeants, Ramsden and Whitaker, searched Thwaites's home but found no knife. They found a puppy, a bed recently slept in, and on the table, a long signed confession from the young man who worked as a painter and paper-hanger at Robinson's....'

As an example of how a story like this can be amplified as time goes on, not only was the crime featured in my book, but also emerged again in a family history magazine article when someone discovered the murder story in their work on their own family story.

Keith Henson's volume on York in the same series has a feature on 'A Policeman's Lot' and in that we have an example of how the regional crime books can often supply the kind of social history in which police work was embedded. Some of the experiences recorded in that chapter give excellent examples of the kinds of stories in which your ancestor may have been involved. At the most violent end of the spectrum of police work we have Constable Carter, who was 'set upon by four men and given a severe beating, leaving him " a dreadful picture of brutality". The men were never identified and no motive given, other than he was a policeman' Henson writes. Then we have a full account of P C Cowton, who policed the rough area of the Bedern. Cowton was formerly an inmate of the workhouse, but joined the constabulary in 1852 and lived in the Bedern community with his wife and six children. Henson described one of his fairly regular confrontations in this way: ' Cowton was called at 1 a.m. to break up an argument that had turned violent. He found the whole neighbourhood in the alley, but alone he entered the affray and tried to disperse it. Tempers flared and one man threatened Cowton's life. Luckily, another policeman arrived and the two of them chased who they believed were the ringleaders...'

It may be seen from these examples that a little time spent with volumes of regional crime casebooks may well be something that opens up the most memorable moment of an ancestor's police career. After all, the 'foul deeds' of the books include exactly the kinds of offences recorded in the police charge books, the most common in the mid-Victorian years being vagrancy, poaching, drunkenness, assault, larceny, cruelty to animals and threatening behaviour. But where a simple line in the listings of a charge book may include the officer's name, the fuller account in a casebook gives you the fruits of the research done by the crime historian.

As these volumes are usually chronological in order of presentation, they also give the researcher a useful picture of the development of police work in the city or town the ancestor worked in, and the usual photographs add even more detail, bringing to life the working conditions around the officer's daily life.

Other useful sources
The Times Digital Archive
The Guardian Archive
Magazines:
Master Detective
Murder Most Foul
True Crime
True Detective

Web Sites
Back to Billington families in Lancs.   www.users.bigpond.com/telglen
York Castle Prisons:
www.richard.clark32.btinternet.co.uk/york
The British Female Hanged   ditto

Paul R Williams The Ultimate Price: The Unlawful Killing of English Police Officers
See: www.murderfiles.com

Organisations
The Crime Writers Association   www.thecwa.co.uk
The Police History Society   www.policehistorysociety.co.uk